MY REVISION NOTES

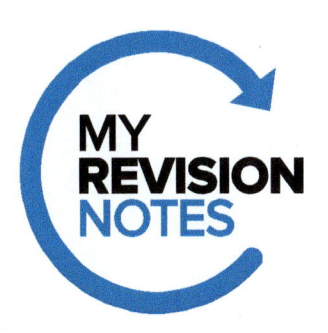

AQA A-level

POLITICS
UK POLITICS

SECOND EDITION

Rowena Hammal and Simon Lemieux

HODDER EDUCATION
AN HACHETTE UK COMPANY

Every effort has been made to trace all copyright holders, but if any have been inadvertently overlooked, the Publishers will be pleased to make the necessary arrangements at the first opportunity.

Although every effort has been made to ensure that website addresses are correct at time of going to press, Hodder Education cannot be held responsible for the content of any website mentioned in this book. It is sometimes possible to find a relocated web page by typing in the address of the home page for a website in the URL window of your browser.

Hachette UK's policy is to use papers that are natural, renewable and recyclable products and made from wood grown in well-managed forests and other controlled sources. The logging and manufacturing processes are expected to conform to the environmental regulations of the country of origin.

Orders: please contact Hachette UK Distribution, Hely Hutchinson Centre, Milton Road, Didcot, Oxfordshire, OX11 7HH. Telephone: +44 (0)1235 827827. Email education@hachette.co.uk. Lines are open from 9 a.m. to 5 p.m., Monday to Friday. You can also order through our website: www.hoddereducation.co.uk

ISBN: 978 1 3983 5530 9

© Rowena Hammal and Simon Lemieux 2022

First published in 2019
This edition published in 2022 by
Hodder Education,
An Hachette UK Company
Carmelite House
50 Victoria Embankment
London EC4Y 0DZ

www.hoddereducation.co.uk

Impression number   5 4 3 2

Year   2026 2025 2024 2023

All rights reserved. Apart from any use permitted under UK copyright law, no part of this publication may be reproduced or transmitted in any form or by any means, electronic or mechanical, including photocopying and recording, or held within any information storage and retrieval system, without permission in writing from the publisher or under licence from the Copyright Licensing Agency Limited. Further details of such licences (for reprographic reproduction) may be obtained from the Copyright Licensing Agency Limited, www.cla.co.uk

Cover photo © Vlad - stock.adobe.com

Illustrations by Integra Software Services Pvt. Ltd, Pondicherry, India

Typeset by Integra Software Services Pvt. Ltd, Pondicherry, India

Printed by CPI Group (UK) Ltd, Croydon CR0 4YY

A catalogue record for this title is available from the British Library.

Get the most from this book

Everyone has to decide their own revision strategy, but it is essential to review your work, learn it and test your understanding. These Revision Notes will help you to do that in a planned way, topic by topic. Use this book as the cornerstone of your revision and do not hesitate to write in it — personalise your notes and check your progress by ticking off each section as you revise.

Tick to track your progress

Use the revision planner on pages 4 and 5 to plan your revision, topic by topic. Tick each box when you have:
+ revised and understood the topic
+ tested yourself
+ practised the exam questions and gone online to check your answers and complete the quick quizzes.

You can also keep track of your revision by ticking off each topic heading in the book. You may find it helpful to add your own notes as you work through each topic.

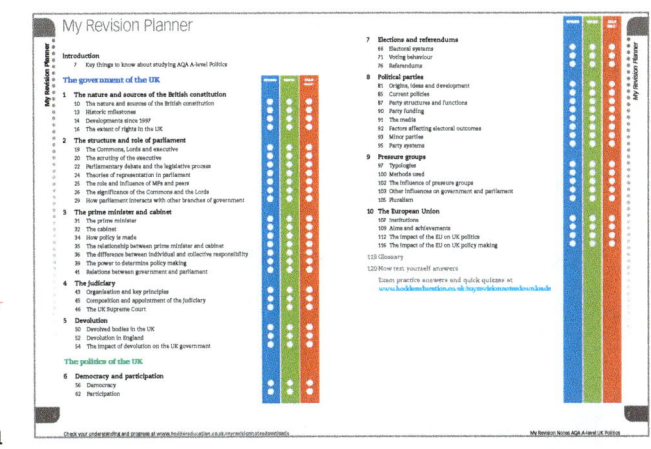

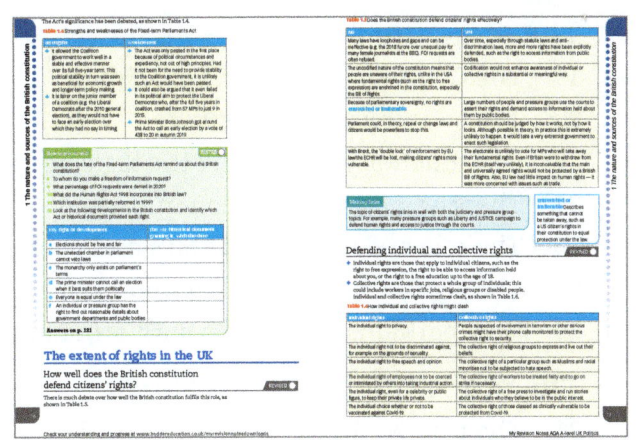

Features to help you succeed

Exam tips
Expert tips are given throughout the book to help you polish your exam technique in order to maximise your chances in the exam.

Now test yourself
These short, knowledge-based questions provide the first step in testing your learning. Answers are given at the back of the book.

Exam practice
Practice exam questions are provided for each topic. Use them to consolidate your revision and practise your exam skills. Note that 25-mark A-level exam practice questions can also be used as AS practice questions.

Revision activities
These activities will help you to understand each topic in an interactive way.

Making links
This feature identifies specific connections between topics and tells you how revising these will aid your exam answers.

Key words
Clear, concise definitions of essential key terms are provided where they first appear.

Summaries
The summaries provide a quick-check bullet list for each topic.

Online
Go online to check your answers to the exam questions at **www.hoddereducation.co.uk/myrevisionnotesdownloads**

My Revision Notes AQA A-level UK Politics Second Edition

My Revision Planner

Introduction
7 Key things to know about studying AQA A-level Politics

The government of the UK

1 The nature and sources of the British constitution
- 10 The nature and sources of the British constitution
- 13 Historic milestones
- 14 Developments since 1997
- 16 The extent of rights in the UK

2 The structure and role of parliament
- 19 The Commons, Lords and executive
- 20 The scrutiny of the executive
- 22 Parliamentary debate and the legislative process
- 24 Theories of representation in parliament
- 25 The role and influence of MPs and peers
- 26 The significance of the Commons and the Lords
- 29 How parliament interacts with other branches of government

3 The prime minister and cabinet
- 31 The prime minister
- 32 The cabinet
- 34 How policy is made
- 35 The relationship between prime minister and cabinet
- 36 The difference between individual and collective responsibility
- 39 The power to determine policy making
- 41 Relations between government and parliament

4 The judiciary
- 43 Organisation and key principles
- 45 Composition and appointment of the judiciary
- 46 The UK Supreme Court

5 Devolution
- 50 Devolved bodies in the UK
- 52 Devolution in England
- 54 The impact of devolution on the UK government

The politics of the UK

6 Democracy and participation
- 56 Democracy
- 62 Participation

Check your understanding and progress at www.hoddereducation.co.uk/myrevisionnotesdownloads

7 Elections and referendums
- 66 Electoral systems
- 71 Voting behaviour
- 76 Referendums

8 Political parties
- 81 Origins, ideas and development
- 85 Current policies
- 87 Party structures and functions
- 90 Party funding
- 91 The media
- 92 Factors affecting electoral outcomes
- 93 Minor parties
- 95 Party systems

9 Pressure groups
- 97 Typologies
- 100 Methods used
- 102 The influence of pressure groups
- 103 Other influences on government and parliament
- 105 Pluralism

10 The European Union
- 107 Institutions
- 109 Aims and achievements
- 112 The impact of the EU on UK politics
- 116 The impact of the EU on UK policy making

119 Glossary

124 Now test yourself answers

Exam practice answers available at
www.hoddereducation.co.uk/myrevisionnotesdownloads

Countdown to my exams

6–8 weeks to go

- Start by looking at the specification — make sure you know exactly what material you need to revise and the style of the examination.
- Use the revision planner on pages 4 and 5 to familiarise yourself with the topics.
- Organise your notes, making sure you have covered everything on the specification. The revision planner will help you to group your notes into topics.
- Work out a realistic revision plan that will allow you time for relaxation. Set aside days and times for all the subjects that you need to study, and stick to your timetable.
- Set yourself sensible targets. Break your revision down into focused sessions of around 40 minutes, divided by breaks. These Revision Notes organise the basic facts into short, memorable sections to make revising easier.

REVISED

2–6 weeks to go

- Read through the relevant sections of this book and refer to the exam tips, summaries and key words. Tick off the topics as you feel confident about them. Highlight those topics you find difficult and look at them again in detail.
- Test your understanding of each topic by working through the 'Now test yourself' questions and 'Revision activities' in the book. Look up the answers at the back of the book.
- Make a note of any problem areas as you revise, and ask your teacher to go over these in class.
- Look at past papers. They are one of the best ways to revise and practise your exam skills. Write or prepare planned answers to the exam practice questions provided in this book. Check your answers online at **www.hoddereducation.co.uk/myrevisionnotesdownloads**
- Try different revision methods. For example, you can make notes using mind maps, spider diagrams or flashcards.
- Track your progress using the revision planner and give yourself a reward when you have achieved your target.

REVISED

One week to go

- Try to fit in at least one more timed practice of an entire past paper and seek feedback from your teacher, comparing your work closely with the mark scheme.
- Check the revision planner to make sure you haven't missed out any topics. Brush up on any areas of difficulty by talking them over with a friend or getting help from your teacher.
- Attend any revision classes put on by your teacher. Remember, they are an expert at preparing people for examinations.

REVISED

The day before the examination

- Flick through these Revision Notes for useful reminders, for example the exam tips and key words.
- Check the time and place of your examination.
- Make sure you have everything you need — extra pens and pencils, tissues, a watch, bottled water, sweets.
- Allow some time to relax and have an early night to ensure you are fresh and alert for the examinations.

REVISED

Check your understanding and progress at www.hoddereducation.co.uk/myrevisionnotesdownloads

Introduction

Key things to know about studying AQA A-level Politics

This book covers all of Paper 1, Government and Politics of the UK. Government and politics of the USA and comparative politics, and Political Ideas — Papers 2 and 3, respectively — are covered in two other My Revision Notes series books.

As a student of A-level Politics, it is important that you know these five things about the examination:
+ The structure of the exam
+ The three assessment objectives
+ The command words 'explain', 'analyse', 'compare' and 'evaluate', and what these terms mean
+ The format of the extract-based essay question — Section B
+ The synoptic element for Section C.

The structure of the exam

Paper 1: Government and Politics of the UK (two hours):
+ Section A: Answer **all** three shorter-answer questions (27 marks)
+ Section B Answer the extract-based question (25 marks)
+ Section C: Answer **one** essay question from a choice of two (25 marks).

Remember that Paper 1 is worth one-third of your A-level, so divide your revision time up evenly across all three papers.

Assessment objectives

Your answers will be marked by examiners who will look to see how well you have met the three assessment objectives. These are explained below.

> **Assessment objectives**
>
> AO1: Knowledge and understanding
> + Identify/provide points related to the question.
> + Offer relevant examples, both recent and more historic.
> + Use relevant and appropriate political terminology.
>
> AO2: Analysis
> + Give a two-sided, balanced debate in essays and the extract-based question.
> + Comment upon and explain any points made.
>
> AO3: Evaluation
> + Distinguish between strong and weak arguments, explicitly identify which arguments/factors are most convincing and why.
> + Provide reasons for the judgements made.

Command words explained for Section A

In Section A, the questions will start with the following words: 'Explain and analyse three reasons/factors/arguments why …'

+ **Explain** means to identify and describe a factor, giving an example or two, and then comment briefly on it.
+ **Analyse** is a pretty open term. It involves taking your answer beyond a simple explanation by examining the factor critically rather than just taking it at face value. Is it, for example, a factor that has become more/less important recently? How significant a factor is it? Perhaps think of it as responding to the examiner's reaction of 'so what?' after you have explained/described a factor.

Command words explained for Section B

In the source-based question, the arguments that are used in your answer will come from the source that is provided. The extract(s) will contain points on both sides of a debate, such as reforming the electoral system.

You will be asked to analyse, evaluate and compare the arguments in the extract(s).

+ **Analyse** requires the same approach/skills as for Section A questions.
+ **Evaluate** means to make a judgement. For exam purposes, this usually means that you need to 'decide' or make a 'judgement call' on the strength of the arguments and points contained in the extract(s). It means that you need to weigh up the different arguments considered, including relevant political perspectives, and clearly state which is the most convincing and why. This should happen throughout the essay after you have analysed an argument, not just in the conclusion.
+ **Compare** requires you to identify and explain the key points on both sides of the debate/argument.

Additional points for the Section B extract-based essay question

+ The text is usually a short extract, often two, that contains points on both sides of a debate. The extracts may be by the same author or written by different authors. The date, source and perhaps some detail about the provenance (who wrote it) will be provided.
+ The extract(s) need to be briefly but relevantly evaluated for accuracy/bias. Consider aspects such as who wrote it, their purpose, and when they wrote it, for example whether it was just before or after a key event happened that affected the topic in the question. If so, can you explain how this limits the extract's understanding of the issue in question? If you know the political perspective of the author(s), or the organisation they are writing for, you might comment on how this could influence their view of the topic in question.
+ Your answer needs to be focused on the question at all times. Use mini quotes to highlight key points in the text and then analyse and evaluate them.
+ All points made in the extract(s) need to be evaluated using your own wider knowledge. This knowledge might support or weaken the point — it doesn't matter which — but do not just rely on points/details contained in the extract(s).
+ Your conclusion needs to clearly explain which side of the argument is more convincing and why.

Check your understanding and progress at www.hoddereducation.co.uk/myrevisionnotesdownloads

Command words explained for the Section C essay question

All essay questions will contain a statement that you will be asked to **analyse** and **evaluate**. Refer to the points above for what these command terms mean.

Additional points for the Section C essay question

+ Stay focused throughout on the content contained in the statement and avoid writing a generalised essay.
+ Identify key themes, perhaps three or four, and analyse and evaluate each one in turn, reaching a mini conclusion that directly relates back to the statement in the title.
+ Ensure that a clear and relevant conclusion is reached at the end that is consistent with the overall line of argument throughout the essay.
+ For the Section C essay, you will need to refer, at least briefly, to content covered in other Paper 1, 2 or 3 topics. These are officially termed **synoptic links** in the exam specification. This should occur quite naturally; for example, an essay about the limits to prime ministerial power is naturally likely to include knowledge gained from your study of parliament and/or the judiciary, and perhaps the US president, and so on.

1 The nature and sources of the British constitution

Key points

+ A constitution is essentially the rulebook by which a country is governed. It sets out the various powers and responsibilities of each branch of government, as well as laying out the rights and civil liberties of all citizens.
+ Constitutions come in all shapes and sizes. Authoritarian dictatorships such as North Korea and the former Soviet Union, as well as Western democracies, have constitutions.

The nature and sources of the British constitution

Nature

Every country's constitution has its own unique characteristics and origins, and Britain is no exception. Table 1.1 identifies the key terms that define the British constitution.

Table 1.1 Defining the British constitution

Key term	Definition and key facts	Significance
Uncodified	+ The British constitution is found in a variety of sources, meaning it is uncodified. + Few other countries have an uncodified constitution. Those that do include Saudi Arabia and New Zealand.	+ It can make it more difficult for British subjects to understand their rights and how their political system works. + It can make it easier to adapt, e.g. by Acts of Parliament, as no complicated procedures are required to amend it.
Unitary	+ All power ultimately derives from central government. + This is the opposite of a federal constitution (e.g. the USA).	+ The Westminster Parliament is sovereign and therefore very powerful. + Any power given to the regions (e.g. through devolution) is delegated, not transferred permanently.
Rule of law	+ Everyone is equally subject to the laws of the land. + Even governments and ministers cannot break their own laws. + Described by AV Dicey as one of the 'twin pillars' of the constitution. + The opposite of arbitrary government, commonly associated with dictatorships.	+ Identifies Britain as a modern liberal democracy. + Ensures the powers of government are limited. + If a government or government department is found to have broken their own rules or guidelines, they are deemed to have acted *ultra vires*, i.e. beyond the power of the law. + It can lead to the government having to reverse an action, e.g. in 2019 Prime Minister Boris Johnson was found by the courts to have acted illegally by attempting to prorogue (suspend) parliament for five weeks without its consent during the Brexit debates.
Parliamentary sovereignty	+ Parliament is the supreme authority in the land; the constitution is what parliament says it is and it can be altered at will by statute law. + This contrasts with countries such as the USA, which are said to embody constitutional sovereignty whereby government and legislature must follow the constitution when passing laws. No such requirement exists in Britain. Parliamentary sovereignty is the other of AV Dicey's 'twin pillars'.	+ This is a fundamental and ancient principle of the British constitution. + It means it is flexible and easy to change, as all it takes is for parliament to pass a law to change the constitution. + No parliament can bind its successor, meaning that the constitution can be changed and even reversed over time. + Shown by laws both to join the EU originally (1972) and subsequently to leave it (2020).

Check your understanding and progress at www.hoddereducation.co.uk/myrevisionnotesdownloads

> **Exam tips**
>
> Students often write that the British constitution is unwritten, but this is not accurate. Rather, it is uncodified, and found written down in various sources.
>
> Although it is right to say that the British constitution as a whole is uncodified, some parts of it have been 'micro-codified'. For example, the Equality Act 2010 brought together and thus codified several existing pieces of anti-discrimination law such as the Equal Pay Act 1970 and the Disability Discrimination Act 1995.

Parliamentary sovereignty The basis of the UK constitution. Parliament is the supreme authority in Britain. This means that parliament's laws cannot be struck down by a higher authority.

Sources

REVISED

As mentioned above, the British constitution derives from several sources, as shown in Figure 1.1 and Table 1.2.

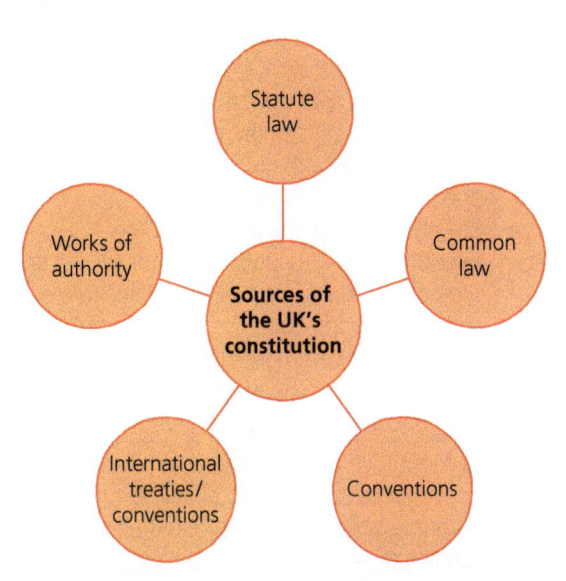

Figure 1.1 The UK's uncodified constitution

Table 1.2 The sources of the British constitution

Source	Definition and key facts	Significance
Statute law	+ Acts of Parliament that affect and alter the British constitution. They can cover laws about who can vote, such as the Great Reform Act 1832, and how elections are run (the Ballot Act 1872). + It covers laws that impact on civil liberties and **human rights**, such as the Human Rights Act 1998, which incorporated the European Convention on Human Rights (ECHR) into UK law.	+ The British constitution remains flexible and adaptable. + The trend has been towards expanding and protecting democracy and individual rights, e.g. giving all women the vote by 1928. + In theory, these rights could be removed or diluted if parliament so desired. In reality, many currently have the 'double lock' of additional backing from the ECHR.
Common law	+ Laws passed down over the years by legal judgments in the courts. + Represents judicial precedence. Examples include the right to free expression and the defence of property rights. + Some key historical documents such as Magna Carta are based on common law not statute law.	+ Does not have precedence over statute law/Acts of Parliament. + Statute law can repeal or modify rights granted under common law. For example, although the rights of property owners can be found in various ancient documents, statute laws — such as those dealing with compulsory purchase orders — modify these ancient rights.

1 The nature and sources of the British constitution

My Revision Notes AQA A-level UK Politics Second Edition

1 The nature and sources of the British constitution

Source	Definition and key facts	Significance
Royal prerogative	+ The historic political powers of the monarch, now effectively transferred to the prime minister. + As an example, although technically the armed forces are those of the monarch, in reality decisions about deployment and size are made by the government not the sovereign.	+ It is often cited as a way that governments can extend their powers, e.g. honours including peerages can be handed out by the prime minister alone. + It can be limited by Acts of Parliament, e.g. the Fixed-term Parliaments Act 2011.
Conventions	+ Unwritten traditions that help to 'oil the wheels' of state and enable government and political activity to run more smoothly. + A good example is the 1945 Salisbury-Addison Convention whereby the Lords agreed not to delay policies contained in the governing party's **manifesto**.	+ These normally work well, e.g. they enabled David Cameron to have the first chance to form a coalition government after the indecisive result of the 2010 general election. + Conventions are not protected by anything more substantial than tradition. If a convention is to work properly, there must be a shared understanding of what it means. A contested convention is not a convention at all. + When the Lords rejected the People's Budget in 1909 and broke convention, a constitutional crisis took place. + Strictly speaking, the passage of the legislation enabling Brexit to happen reflects the convention that parliament bows to the will of the people following a referendum result. The government was not legally or constitutionally obliged to implement the outcome of the 2016 referendum.
Authoritative opinions	+ The writings and books of constitutional experts that clarify and explain the inner workings of the constitution. + Examples include AV Dicey's *Introduction to the Study of the Law of the Constitution* and Walter Bagehot's *The English Constitution*. + Also comprise more recent sources such as the Cabinet Manual (2010), which set out the main laws, rules and conventions affecting the conduct and operation of the government.	+ Authoritative opinions are rather like conventions and have no absolute legal authority but nonetheless help the smooth running of government. + Not usually approved formally by parliament and can be changed easily. + Embody and describe existing rules and conventions, and do not seek to change them. + A good example is when Bagehot made the famous distinction between the 'dignified' and the 'efficient' parts of the constitution.
International treaties and conventions	+ Treaties or agreements that the UK government has signed up to, such as the European Convention on Human Rights (ECHR).	+ A prime example is the ECHR, which all parliamentary legislation must conform with. This has implications in policy areas such as asylum law. Topics such as environmental controls are also affected, for example by the UK having signed the 2015 Paris Agreement on climate change.

> **Human rights** Those rights that apply to all people. They are absolute, universal and fundamental. They cannot be removed from anyone.
>
> **Royal prerogative** The powers traditionally held by the monarch but now, in practice, the preserve of the prime minister. These include the power of patronage, being commander-in-chief and negotiating treaties with foreign powers.
>
> **Manifesto** A list of policy commitments released by a party before an election. Once elected, a government should deliver its manifesto.

> **Making links**
>
> The statute laws expanding the franchise affected the constitution, but also represented the growth of universal suffrage, which is covered in Chapter 6 on democracy and participation.

Check your understanding and progress at www.hoddereducation.co.uk/myrevisionnotesdownloads

Historic milestones

Magna Carta (1215)

REVISED

- An agreement between King John and his barons that established the principle that everyone, including the king, was subject to the law.
- Above all, it established the principle of the right to a fair trial.
- Although re-issued and partly altered in the following decades, Magna Carta is nonetheless seen as a landmark document in the development of human rights. Some clauses have found their way into other key documents such as the American Bill of Rights (1791) and the Universal Declaration of Human Rights (1948).
- Note that Magna Carta did not give many rights to ordinary people.

Bill of Rights (1689)

REVISED

- Another agreement between the king and parliament.
- Stated that parliaments must meet frequently, elections must be free and there must be complete freedom of speech within parliament — known as parliamentary privilege.
- Also included the principle of no taxation without parliament's agreement.
- Effectively created and embodied the notion of parliamentary sovereignty.

> **Parliamentary privilege** The right of **MPs** to free speech within the Palace of Westminster. They cannot be sued for slander or contempt of court. This is significant as it enables MPs to speak freely in parliament. One example was in July 2021 when SDLP MP Colum Eastwood used it to name 'Soldier F', a British soldier accused of involvement in the 1972 Bloody Sunday shootings in Northern Ireland.
>
> **MPs** Members of Parliament, each representing a geographical area of the UK known as a constituency (650 total), who sit in the House of Commons. The average number of voters per MP is 68,000, although the largest constituency, the Isle of Wight, has over 100,000 voters.

Act of Settlement (1701)

REVISED

- Only Protestants, not Roman Catholics, could become the monarch or be married to the monarch, which guaranteed the Protestant succession.
- Its constitutional importance lies not in its anti-Catholic bias, but rather in what it said about the relative power of Crown and parliament.
- Asserted parliament's dominant position since direct hereditary succession was decreed less significant than religious affiliation.
- Established the fundamental principle that the monarchy existed on parliament's terms, not vice versa.

Parliament Acts (1911 and 1949)

REVISED

- Significantly reduced the rights and powers of the unelected House of Lords.
- The 1911 Act removed their power of absolute veto over legislation and limited their power to that of a two-year delay.
- The 1949 Act reduced the delay to just one year.
- Both Acts increased the powers of the Commons over the House of Lords.

European Communities Act (1972)

REVISED

- Brought in by the Conservative government of Edward Heath and marked the entry of the UK into what is now the EU.

- Constitutionally it represented a weakening of parliamentary sovereignty as all British law had to conform to and comply with EU law.
- Areas it impacted included the ability of the government to control immigration from other EU countries and to make trade deals with non-EU countries.
- The 2016 Brexit vote shows how this major impact on the constitution can be undone.
- Although the original 1972 Act weakened the rights of parliament to pass its own laws, subsequent events since 2016 have enabled parliamentary sovereignty to come to the fore again. What a parliament in 1972 created, a twenty-first-century parliament can unmake!

> **Exam tip**
>
> If writing an answer about how well the British constitution defends rights and liberties, do not confuse the Bill of Rights (1689) with later human rights legislation. The 1689 Act was about asserting the power of parliament over the monarchy, not about key individual rights. Elections might well have been required to be free and regular, but most people did not have the vote in 1689.

Now test yourself

1. Why does the Brexit vote highlight parliamentary sovereignty?
2. The Bill of Rights established what important principle dealing with MPs' freedom of speech?
3. Since 1949, what is the maximum length of time the Lords can delay a bill for?
4. What document sets out how governments today should run?
5. Does a convention have legal backing?
6. What are the three features of a human right?

Answers on p. 124

Developments since 1997

Recent developments

- The British constitution has evolved and developed over the centuries.
- Major reforms in the nineteenth and early twentieth centuries expanded who could vote and changed the conduct of elections; more recent changes have focused on strengthening individual and collective rights, and the country's relationship with the EU.
- There have been some lesser changes to parliament itself and to the power of the prime minister. Tony Blair's Labour government, which was first elected in 1997, made constitutional reform a major part of their legislative agenda.

Among recent developments of the constitution are:

- the creation and expansion of powers in the devolved assemblies/parliaments in Scotland, Wales and Northern Ireland, such as the Wales Act 2014 and 2017, and the Scotland Act 2016
- a major reform in the composition of the House of Lords in 1999, with the removal of most hereditary peers, leaving just 92 in place
- the Human Rights Act 1998
- laws that enhance individual rights, such as the Freedom of Information Act 2000, the Data Protection Act 1998 and its successor, the General Data Protection Regulation 2018, and the Fixed-term Parliaments Act 2011
- the European Union (Withdrawal) Act 2018.

> **Peers** Members of the House of Lords, mostly life peers who have been nominated by political leaders over the years, along with 92 hereditary peers and 26 Church of England bishops.

> **Exam tip**
>
> Do not confuse EU law and the European Convention on Human Rights (ECHR). The ECHR refers to general rights, such as the right to a family life. It stems from Britain's membership of the Council of Europe, a completely separate body to the EU. Although a country must be in the Council of Europe to join the EU, a country not in the EU (e.g. Norway) can belong to the Council of Europe and must also abide by the ECHR. The Human Rights Act 1998 incorporated the ECHR into British law and is unaffected by Brexit.

Check your understanding and progress at www.hoddereducation.co.uk/myrevisionnotesdownloads

Significance of recent developments

REVISED

Freedom of Information Act 2000

This Act requires public bodies such as government departments, local authorities and the NHS to:
+ publish and make publicly available certain information about their activities, such as an annual report and minutes of meetings
+ allow members of the public to request information from these public authorities via a freedom of information (FOI) request.

The Act is designed to promote openness and transparency among public bodies that benefit from taxpayers' money. It is also meant to boost public trust in such organisations and remove shrouds of secrecy. Its workings are overseen by the independent Information Commissioner's Office (ICO).

Some strengths and weaknesses of the Freedom of Information Act are given in Table 1.3.

> **Exam tip**
>
> If you are answering a question about the significance of any one or two constitutional changes since 1997, make sure that you do not just describe the change but also analyse it: how well has it worked and what are its strengths and drawbacks?

Table 1.3 Strengths and weaknesses of the Freedom of Information Act

Strengths	Weaknesses
+ FOI requests are popular and widespread; over 44,000 such requests were made in 2020 alone. + It allows the public and **pressure groups** to identify possible examples of waste and inefficiency or, at worst, corruption in public bodies. + It is an important investigative tool for journalists, prising open information that those in power might prefer to remain hidden. For example, the Act played a significant role in uncovering the MPs' expenses scandal in 2009. + It can also be used by businesses. For example, in 2021 an FOI request about jewellery thefts was made to UK police forces by the retailer jewellerybox. It showed that in 2020 the largest number occurred in Kensington & Chelsea, with 967 cases of jewellery thefts. + It allows public scrutiny of policy initiatives and how well they work in practice. For example, in 2006 there was a highly publicised knife amnesty. An FOI request forced the publication of a report into the impact of the amnesty by the Metropolitan Police. This showed it had minimal impact on the rates of knife-related crime. + Those initially denied access to the requested information can appeal to the Information Commissioner's Office (ICO). There were 311 such appeals in 2019/20.	+ Public bodies can and often do refuse requests for information. This can be for a variety of reasons including national security, commercial sensitivity, cost or because the request is deemed 'vexatious'. + In 2020 around 50% of all requests were declined, either in full or in part. + It is often the case that requests for information are declined because they would involve the release of private or personal information about individuals. The Act can therefore lead to a conflict between an individual's right to privacy and the right of the public to gain access to information about public officials.

Fixed-term Parliaments Act 2011

+ Passed following the formation of the Coalition government between the Conservatives and Liberal Democrats after the 2010 general election.
+ Weakened the power of the prime minister to call a snap election by dissolving parliament unilaterally.
+ Parliament now needs to vote by a two-thirds majority to call an early general election. Alternatively, if there is a vote of no confidence in the government, this must be confirmed by another vote within two weeks.
+ Designed to enhance the stability of a potentially fragile coalition government and reduce the scope for the prime minister to gain political advantage by going to the polls when the chances of victory seem highest.
+ Following the Conservatives' 2019 manifesto pledge, the Act was due to be repealed in 2021. Labour had also promised to repeal the Act if elected in 2019.

> **Pressure groups**
>
> Organisations that campaign for a specific cause, such as a trade union or an environmental cause. Unlike a political party, pressure groups generally do not aim to win political power through elections.

The Act's significance has been debated, as shown in Table 1.4.

Table 1.4 Strengths and weaknesses of the Fixed-term Parliaments Act

Strengths	Weaknesses
+ It allowed the Coalition government to work well in a stable and effective manner over its full five-year term. This political stability in turn was seen as beneficial for economic growth and longer-term policy making. + It is fairer on the junior member of a coalition (e.g. the Liberal Democrats after the 2010 general election), as they would not have to face an early election over which they had no say in timing.	+ The Act was only passed in the first place because of political circumstances and expediency, not out of high principles. Had it not been for the need to provide stability to the Coalition government, it is unlikely such an Act would have been passed. + It could also be argued that it even failed in its political aim to protect the Liberal Democrats who, after the full five years in coalition, crashed from 57 MPs to just 9 in 2015. + Prime Minister Boris Johnson got around the Act to call an early election by a vote of 438 to 20 in autumn 2019.

> **Now test yourself** TESTED
>
> 7 What does the fate of the Fixed-term Parliaments Act remind us about the British constitution?
> 8 To whom do you make a freedom of information request?
> 9 What percentage of FOI requests were denied in 2020?
> 10 What did the Human Rights Act 1998 incorporate into British law?
> 11 Which institution was partially reformed in 1999?
> 12 Look at the following developments in the British constitution and identify which Act or historical document provided each right.
>
> | Key right or development | The Act/historical document granting it, with the date |
> |---|---|
> | a Elections should be free and fair | |
> | b The unelected chamber in parliament cannot veto laws | |
> | c The monarchy only exists on parliament's terms | |
> | d The prime minister cannot call an election when it best suits them politically | |
> | e Everyone is equal under the law | |
> | f An individual or pressure group has the right to find out reasonable details about government departments and public bodies | |
>
> Answers on p. 124

The extent of rights in the UK

How well does the British constitution defend citizens' rights?

REVISED

There is much debate over how well the British constitution fulfils this role, as shown in Table 1.5.

Table 1.5 Does the British constitution defend citizens' rights effectively?

No	Yes
Many laws have loopholes and gaps and can be ineffective (e.g. the 2018 furore over unequal pay for many female journalists at the BBC). FOI requests are often refused.	Over time, especially through statute laws and anti-discrimination laws, more and more rights have been explicitly defended, such as the right to access information from public bodies.
The uncodified nature of the constitution means that people are unaware of their rights, unlike in the USA where fundamental rights (such as the right to free expression) are enshrined in the constitution, especially the Bill of Rights.	Codification would not enhance awareness of individual or collective rights in a substantial or meaningful way.
Because of parliamentary sovereignty, no rights are **entrenched or inalienable**.	Large numbers of people and pressure groups use the courts to assert their rights and demand access to information held about them by public bodies.
Parliament could, in theory, repeal or change laws and citizens would be powerless to stop this.	A constitution should be judged by how it works, not by how it looks. Although possible in theory, in practice this is extremely unlikely to happen. It would take a very extremist government to enact such legislation.
With Brexit, the 'double lock' of reinforcement by EU law/the ECHR will be lost, making citizens' rights more vulnerable.	The electorate is unlikely to vote for MPs who will take away their fundamental rights. Even if Britain were to withdraw from the ECHR (itself very unlikely), it is inconceivable that the main and universally agreed rights would not be protected by a British Bill of Rights. Also, EU law had little impact on human rights — it was more concerned with issues such as trade.

> **Making links**
>
> The topic of citizens' rights links in well with both the judiciary and pressure group topics. For example, many pressure groups such as Liberty and JUSTICE campaign to defend human rights and access to justice through the courts.

> **Entrenched or inalienable** Describes something that cannot be taken away, such as a US citizen's rights in their constitution to equal protection under the law.

Defending individual and collective rights

REVISED

+ Individual rights are those that apply to individual citizens, such as the right to free expression, the right to be able to access information held about you, or the right to a free education up to the age of 18.
+ Collective rights are those that protect a whole group of individuals; this could include workers in specific jobs, religious groups or disabled people. Individual and collective rights sometimes clash, as shown in Table 1.6.

Table 1.6 How individual and collective rights might clash

Individual rights	Collective rights
The individual right to privacy.	People suspected of involvement in terrorism or other serious crimes might have their phone calls monitored to protect the collective right to security.
The individual right not to be discriminated against, for example on the grounds of sexuality.	The collective right of religious groups to express and live out their beliefs.
The individual right to free speech and opinion.	The collective right of a particular group such as Muslims and racial minorities not to be subjected to hate speech.
The individual right of employees not to be coerced or intimidated by others into taking industrial action.	The collective right of workers to be treated fairly and to go on strike if necessary.
The individual right, even for a celebrity or public figure, to keep their private life private.	The collective right of a free press to investigate and run stories about individuals who they believe to be in the public interest.
The individual choice whether or not to be vaccinated against Covid-19.	The collective right of those classed as clinically vulnerable to be protected from Covid-19.

Now test yourself

TESTED

13 Look at the following examples and decide whether each one is primarily about individual or collective rights, briefly explaining why.

	Example	An individual or collective right	Reasons
a	A Christian owner of a bed and breakfast establishment refuses to allow a gay couple to rent a room with a double bed.		
b	Workers for the taxi firm Uber demand to have full employment rights.		
c	A tabloid newspaper learns that a cabinet minister has been conducting an affair and breaking social distancing rules during the Covid-19 pandemic, that they have been urging the public to follow, and wants to publish the story.		
d	An employee with mobility problems asks their firm to locate them in a ground floor office as there are no lifts in the listed building.		
e	A group of parents demand that their children's school changes its uniform policy to allow girls to wear trousers.		

Answers on p. 124

Summary

You should now have an understanding of:
+ what a constitution is and the key terms and characteristics of the British constitution
+ the main sources of the British constitution and key features of each one
+ the main historical milestones in the development of the British constitution and how they impacted its evolution
+ two examples of constitutional change since 1997 and their relative importance
+ how well the British constitution defends individual rights
+ the difference between individual and collective rights, and how and why they can sometimes conflict with each other.

Exam skills

Here is a sample paragraph answering the following Section A, 9-mark question: 'Explain and analyse three ways in which collective and individual rights might clash.'

One way that individual and collective rights might clash is over the issue of compulsion during a public health crisis. For example, during the Covid-19 pandemic, the government made it compulsory for most adults to wear masks in enclosed spaces such as public transport and shops. This placed the individual right whether or not to wear a face mask against the wider collective right to keep the public safe and reduce pressure on the NHS. It also exposed the more complicated issue of conflicting individual rights. For clinically vulnerable citizens, their personal rights – to feel safe when shopping and travelling – clashed with the rights of other individuals whether or not to wear a mask.

This is a strong paragraph as the student directly identifies one way, and then provides a clear and relevant explanation of the ways that collective and individual rights come into conflict. There is also effective analysis at the end where they develop the point that individual rights can also clash. Remember that you will only have around four minutes to write a paragraph — you need to write three paragraphs for each nine-mark question, which should take around 12 minutes or so to write in total. It cannot therefore be too lengthy or detailed.

Exam practice

1 Explain and analyse three key developments of the British constitution after 1900. [9]
2 'Statute law is the best defender of citizens' rights in the UK.' Analyse and evaluate this statement. [25]

Answers available online

Check your understanding and progress at www.hoddereducation.co.uk/myrevisionnotesdownloads

2 The structure and role of parliament

Key points

REVISED

- The UK Parliament is made up of two chambers: the House of Commons and the House of Lords.
  - The House of Commons comprises 650 MPs directly elected at least every five years. The Commons is the dominant house as the 1911 and 1949 Parliament Acts severely limited the powers of the Lords.
  - The House of Lords contains around 800 members. Most are life peers, although 92 hereditary peers remain. There are also 26 senior Church of England bishops.
- Parliament also contains the executive, i.e. all government ministers including the prime minister are either MPs (most) or peers. There is no separation of powers as in the USA.

> **Executive** The government, comprising all ministers and led by the prime minister.

The Commons, Lords and executive

Functions

REVISED

- Parliament is the main law-passing body in the UK, although certain legislative powers are delegated to the devolved assemblies in Scotland, Wales and Northern Ireland. In reality, most laws are actually drawn up by the government and 'rubber-stamped' by parliament after debates and votes.
- One of parliament's key functions is to scrutinise and check the government, though how well and how independently it does this is a matter for debate.
- Parliament is also a forum for representation, both geographic (via constituencies) and political (nearly all MPs belong to a political party).
- Westminster in London is important as a place of national debate, especially in times of national emergency or crisis.
- Increasingly, a lot of the work of parliament is done in committees rather than in the main debating chambers.
- The parliament in Westminster still dominates the UK political process despite devolution, not least since national referendums are used infrequently.

> **Referendums** Direct votes in which the entire electorate is invited to vote on a single political proposal. This may result in the adoption of a new law. In the UK, they are normally used only for major constitutional issues such as EU membership (2016) or changing the electoral system to the Alternative Vote (2011).

> **Exam tip**
> Be cautious when describing parliament as a law-making body; in reality, aside from private members' bills, most laws are drawn up in advance by the government.

> **Making links**
> Voting in referendums is one form of democratic participation. This topic is covered more fully in Chapter 7.

The scrutiny of the executive

How does parliament scrutinise the government?

REVISED

The scrutiny of the executive means checking that the government is carrying out its functions properly. Are its policies working well, is it spending taxpayers' money wisely, how competent and well-informed are ministers? Parliament scrutinises the executive in a number of ways:

+ MPs and peers can ask questions, both written and oral, of government ministers. The best-known example is Prime Minister's Questions (PMQs), which is held at noon on Wednesdays for half an hour.
+ Debates in both chambers allow MPs and peers to air their views about government actions and policies.
+ Departmental select committees investigate and scrutinise actions by civil servants and ministers in each government department, often holding hearings where they can summon witnesses for questioning.
+ Bills go through various stages in parliament, often giving a chance for MPs and peers to suggest changes (amendments) to proposed laws. The committee stage (undertaken by public bill committees) gives an opportunity, away from the main chamber, to go through draft legislation more carefully, clause by clause.
+ Parliament has the final say in all new legislation.
+ A vote of no confidence by the Commons can bring down a government, although this is rare as most governments command a reliable majority in the Commons. The last successful such vote was in March 1979 when James Callaghan's Labour government lost by just one vote.

How effectively parliament scrutinises the executive is considered in Table 2.1.

Table 2.1 How effective is the scrutiny function of parliament?

Method of scrutiny	Advantages	Disadvantages
Prime Minister's Questions (PMQs)	+ They can give positive publicity to the questioner/opposition parties, as when Tony Blair famously accused the then prime minister John Major in January 1997 of being 'weak, weak, weak'. + They allow unwelcome questions to be asked of the prime minister and ministers, and can expose weaknesses, such as when the then prime minister Gordon Brown accidentally said: 'We not only saved the world' when he meant 'saved the banks' during a PMQs exchange. + They keep prime ministers and ministers on their toes. Tony Blair once recalled PMQs as 'the most nerve-racking, discombobulating, nail-biting, bowel-moving, terror-inspiring, courage-draining experience in my prime ministerial life'. + On rare occasions, even members of their own party have criticised the PM during PMQs. Conservative MP David Davis used the quote: 'In the name of God, go' at the height of 'Partygate' in January 2022.	+ They can convey an image of rowdiness and theatricals: 'an exchange of pointless and useless declamations' according to former Labour MP Gerald Kaufman. One such example of this verbal duelling and trying to outsmart one's opponents could be seen in a PMQs session from July 2021 when Prime Minister Boris Johnson attacked Labour and its leader thus: 'We vaccinate, they vacillate. We inoculate, while they're invertebrate.' + In 2014, former Speaker John Bercow wrote to party leaders asking them to help moderate behaviour at PMQs, referring to the atmosphere as often 'very male, very testosterone-fuelled and, in the worst cases, of yobbery and public school twittishness'. + Most questions are designed to either catch out the opposition or praise one's own party, rather than change opinions or policies.

Check your understanding and progress at www.hoddereducation.co.uk/myrevisionnotesdownloads

Method of scrutiny	Advantages	Disadvantages
Parliamentary debates	+ They allow free expression of views and opinions about the issues of the day. + They are televised so the public can watch and be informed. This improves the accessibility and transparency of parliament. + They are an opportunity to change how MPs and peers might vote.	+ Most debates are set-piece occasions; MPs usually adopt the 'party line'. + Many use their speeches to impress their party leadership and further their own career prospects. + Few minds and votes are changed by words spoken in the chamber. Most MPs usually vote along party lines.
Select committees	+ They are less partisan and confrontational than debates and questions in the main chamber. + They are often chaired by MPs from the opposition parties. Yvette Cooper (Labour) chairs the Home Affairs Select Committee. The powerful Public Accounts Committee, which scrutinises value for money across departments, is traditionally chaired by a senior opposition **backbencher** (Meg Hillier in early 2022). + They can call witnesses both from government and outside Westminster to give evidence. On occasion, inaccurate evidence provided by a minister can contribute to their resignation. This happened to Amber Rudd after she inadvertently misled the Home Affairs Select Committee over the Windrush scandal in April 2018. + The government must respond to reports within 60 days. + Reports are often hard-hitting and influential. For example, in May 2018 the Health Select Committee recommended a number of measures to reduce childhood obesity. Within a month, the government announced further measures such as stopping the sale of sweets and fatty snacks at supermarket checkouts.	+ The governing party always has a majority on each committee. + Consensus between parties is not always reached, leading to majority and minority reports along party lines. + Witnesses can be evasive and elusive. + Governments can and do ignore the findings in select committee reports. They only have to respond to and not enact recommendations. For example, in early 2021, the government rejected most of the recommendations regarding Universal Credit made in a report by the Work and Pensions Select Committee, including making a starter payment for all people claiming for the first time rather than waiting five weeks before any benefit payment.
Scrutiny of draft legislation and voting on the final bill	+ Enables bills to be properly checked, amended and discussed. + Parliament can reject the final bill.	+ Strong party loyalty mean a government bill stands little chance of failing. + The governing party has a majority on each public bill committee, so any changes to bills will be minor.
Vote of no confidence	+ The 'nuclear option', which can bring down a government. This happened to Callaghan's Labour government in 1979.	+ Very unlikely to succeed. Only an unstable minority government would be vulnerable. Even the most rebellious MP will be loyal in such a vote.

> **Opposition** MPs and peers not from the governing party or parties. The term 'official opposition' applies specifically to the largest single opposition party. It has its own frontbench shadow cabinet who directly mirror and challenge government ministers, especially at PMQs. Since 1945 the official opposition has always been either the Labour or Conservative party.
>
> **Backbencher** An 'ordinary' MP who is not a government minister or in the shadow cabinet.

Exam tip

Do not confuse public bill committees and departmental select committees. Public bill committees are temporary and exist only for the specific bill they are scrutinising. Select committees are permanent and have a brief to provide wider oversight of government departments and their actions. They do not scrutinise individual pieces of legislation.

> **Now test yourself** TESTED
>
> 1. How many MPs are there in the Commons?
> 2. What religious group does the Lords contain?
> 3. Is parliament best described as law-making or law-passing?
> 4. What is the difference between a select committee and a public bill committee?
> 5. What must a government do with a select committee report?
> 6. Who often chairs select committees?
> 7. What is the chief criticism often levelled at Prime Minister's Questions?
> 8. Why is a vote of no confidence termed the 'nuclear option'?
>
> Answers on p. 124

Parliamentary debate and the legislative process

Parliamentary debate

REVISED

+ Parliamentary debates are one of the main ways MPs, especially those on the opposition benches, get to scrutinise and challenge government policies and bills.
+ They also provide an opportunity for the opposition to say how they would handle matters differently and to project the image of a 'government-in-waiting'.
+ The topics for debate are largely selected by the governing party, but 20 days a year are set aside for opposition parties to choose the subject to be debated. These are known as 'opposition days'. Most bills in parliament get debated at the second reading stage (see Figure 2.1).

The legislative process

REVISED

+ A bill is a proposal for a new law, or a proposal to change an existing law, presented for debate in parliament.
+ A bill can start in the House of Commons or the House of Lords and must pass through the same stages in both houses until it receives royal assent and formally becomes an Act (law).
+ Nearly all government bills will be successful, especially if they are key manifesto pledges.
+ Backbench MPs have the opportunity to introduce their own bills (private members' bills), but these normally rely on government backing if they are to become law.

Main categories

+ Public bills are measures that are universally applicable to all people and organisations. The vast majority of legislation comes under this category.
+ Private bills are usually promoted by organisations including councils and private businesses to give themselves powers beyond, or in conflict with, existing laws. Private bills only change the law for specific individuals or organisations, not the general public. The New Southgate Cemetery Act 2017 is a recent example.
+ Government bills are created and promoted by the government, often to fulfil manifesto promises. All members of the governing party would be expected to support such bills.

> **Royal assent** The formal approval by the monarch of a bill that has successfully passed through parliament and that makes the bill into law. No monarch has refused royal assent since 1707.
>
> **Legislation** The term for all bills that have successfully gone through parliament. A law or Act of Parliament starts off as a bill and only becomes legislation when it has received royal assent.

Check your understanding and progress at www.hoddereducation.co.uk/myrevisionnotesdownloads

> **Making links**
>
> Manifestos are key to understanding the priorities and values of political parties. Find out more about political parties in Chapter 8.

+ Private members' bills are public bills independently introduced by backbench MPs or peers, either as Ten-Minute Rule bills or by being selected as one of 20 'winners' in the annual ballot. Few private members' bills actually become law due to limited time available for debate — only seven were successfully passed in the 2019–21 parliamentary session. Those that do are either non-controversial or receive government backing. One recent example was the 2021 Botulinum Toxin and Cosmetic Fillers (Children) Act, which effectively banned cosmetic Botox treatments for those aged under 18.

> **Exam tip**
>
> Do not confuse private bills and private members' bills. They are not the same thing. Private members' bills are also public bills.

Key stages

The key stages in the passage of a bill through parliament are shown in Figure 2.1.

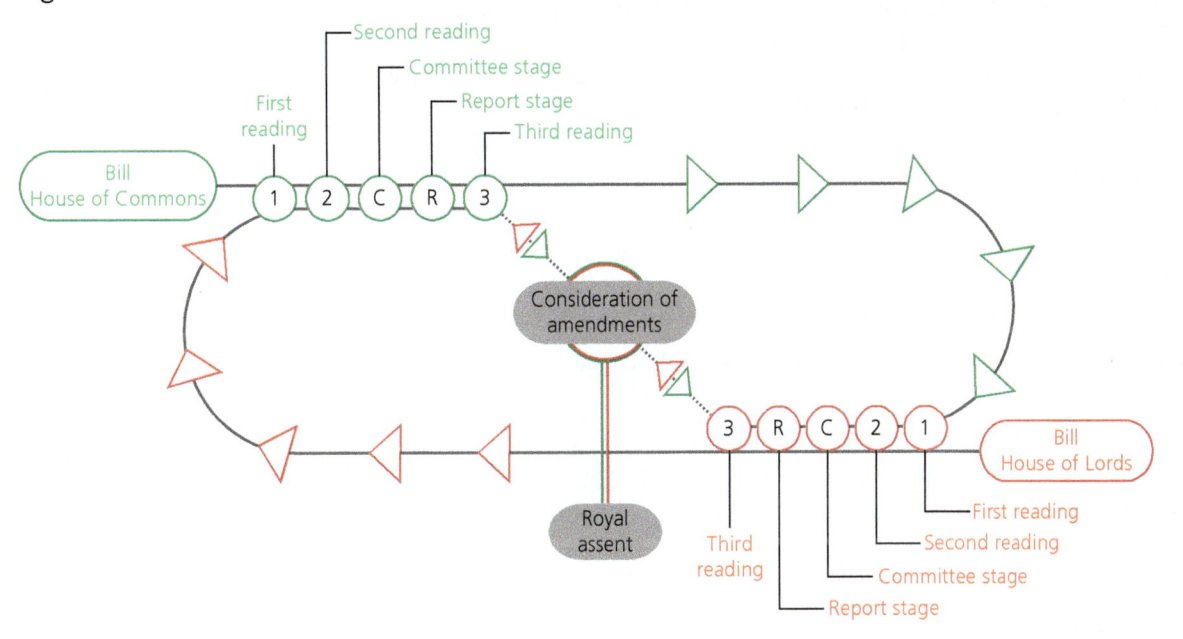

Figure 2.1 Key stages in the legislative process

+ First reading — the bill is formally introduced to parliament. There is no opportunity for debate or a vote.
+ Second reading — the main opportunity for debate, questions and voting on the general principles of a bill. Amendments can also be proposed and voted on. Sometimes, governments can face defeats at this stage. In December 2017, the Commons voted by 309 to 305 to give parliament the final say on the final Brexit deal.
+ Committee stage — a chance to go over the bill and any amendments made in the second reading stage. Each bill is given its own public bill committee comprised of backbench MPs who go over all the clauses in the bill. Major changes are rare as the governing party always has a majority in the committee, but small changes to wording can improve the bill's quality. Pressure groups and individual MPs can submit evidence and address the committee at this stage.
+ Report stage — any changes made at the committee stage are discussed and voted on. This is the last chance for MPs to propose further amendments.
+ Third reading — a short debate. No further changes can be introduced at this stage. A final vote on the bill takes place before it goes for royal assent, provided it has passed through the full stages in both houses.
+ Consideration of amendments — each house considers the other's amendments before the bill goes to the sovereign for royal assent.

The Lords

- The Lords has a key role in revising and amending legislation and can act as a check on the Commons and government. However, the Commons always has the final say. The Lords is best described perhaps as the 'think again' chamber.
- Most bills begin their parliamentary life in the Commons and then go through the same process in the Lords. A few government bills are, however, introduced in the Lords first. These are usually non-controversial, such as the 2021 Air Traffic Management and Unmanned Aircraft Act.
- It is rare for the Lords to reject a bill outright; if they do, the Parliament Act is invoked and the bill automatically becomes law after a year. The Lords can and do make amendments to bills, which are subsequently debated and voted on in the Commons. This often results in bills going back and forth between the two chambers in their final stage — a process informally called 'parliamentary ping-pong'. By itself, the act of delay often causes the government to change course or, on rare occasions, to abandon its plans entirely.
- For example, during the passage of the Internal Markets Bill in 2020, peers voted overwhelmingly to remove a section of the bill that would allow ministers to break international law. The government subsequently removed the relevant clauses in the bill.
- The Lords also has an important function in scrutinising secondary legislation (statutory instruments), which the Commons often lacks the time to do effectively.

> **Now test yourself** TESTED
>
> 9. How important is royal assent in a bill becoming law?
> 10. At what stage in the legislative process is a bill most likely to fail?
> 11. Which stage in the legislative process is described below?
>   a. The best chance to suggest major amendments to a bill.
>   b. The final stage of a bill's progress before becoming law.
>   c. The best opportunity for MPs and interest groups to lobby for specific changes.
>   d. The final vote on a bill.
>   e. When amendments are reviewed and voted upon.
>
> Answers on p. 124

Theories of representation in parliament

The Burkean or trustee model

REVISED

This model is associated with the view of Edmund Burke, an eighteenth-century MP. He argued strongly that electors should entrust their MP with acting in their best interests. He phrased it as: 'Your representative owes you, not his industry only, but his judgement; and he betrays, instead of serving you, if he sacrifices it to your opinion.'

The MP is trusted by their voters to do what they consider is in their constituents' best interests, listening to their views but not being bound by them. It involves exercising their own judgement. An MP voting according to their own conscience, for example over abortion or euthanasia, would be reflecting this model.

The delegate model

REVISED

This is the opposite of the trustee model. MPs are viewed as mouthpieces for their constituents and entirely bound by their wishes. An MP voting against a planning or transport decision that is very unpopular in their constituency would be reflecting this model.

Zac Goldsmith stood down as a Conservative MP and resigned his Richmond Park seat in 2016 to fulfil a promise made to his voters about opposing a third runway for Heathrow. He stood as an independent at the ensuing by-election but was defeated, suggesting that voters may not always reward an MP's adherence to the delegate model.

Mandate theory

REVISED

MPs are elected primarily to carry out the manifesto promises of their party. This is the prevalent model in modern British politics, given the power and discipline of political parties. It reflects the fact that most votes an MP receives are because of party allegiance, not their own personality.

The role and influence of MPs and peers

What role do MPs and peers have?

REVISED

Both MPs and peers may:
+ vote on legislation
+ sit on parliamentary committees
+ serve in the government as a minister or on the opposition frontbench (shadow cabinet)
+ contribute to debates and ask questions of ministers
+ introduce their own bills (private members' bills) to parliament
+ make media appearances and give interviews
+ enjoy parliamentary privilege.

In addition, MPs have the following roles:
+ Undertaking constituency casework: MPs have a duty to serve all their constituents, not merely those who voted for them.
+ Holding regular surgeries: most MPs hold regular surgeries where the public can meet them and raise issues directly with them. This may be lobbying on a particular issue such as a hospital closure or to discuss personal matters such as those relating to housing or immigration.
+ This could be seen as an example of parliament fulfilling its traditional role of redress of grievances. MPs employ constituency caseworkers to handle much of this work.
+ Undertaking backbench rebellions: MPs from the governing party have increasingly been willing to vote against their own government. Recent notable rebellions occurred over aspects of the Brexit process between 2017 and 2019. In September 2019, 21 Conservative MPs lost the whip after they rebelled in one vote that led to the government being defeated. Backbench rebellions are especially effective when a government has a small overall majority, such as the May government (2017–19). They are less effective when the government commands a large majority. For example, although 30 Tory backbenchers rebelled in July 2021 over cuts to the foreign aid budget, the government won the vote.
+ Having a key role in the selection of party leader: both Labour and the Conservatives require leadership candidates to secure a set number of nominations from their sitting MPs before a party membership vote.
+ Providing democratic legitimacy to government.

Lobbying Attempting to influence the actions, policies or decisions of MPs.

Redress of grievances The right of citizens to get wrongs or injustices put right. For example, a constituent might try to get their MP to put pressure on a government department or local council to treat a complaint more fairly. An MP could also do this by asking a parliamentary question or possibly by attempting to bring in a private members' bill to address the issue.

Democratic legitimacy The authority a body (here, the Commons) possesses if it is elected and accountable to the people via free and fair elections.

In addition, peers have the following roles:
+ Contributing specialised insights in debates: peers often come from a wider range of backgrounds such as science, the arts, business and academia than members of the House of Commons, so are able to contribute more specialised insights in debates.
+ Maintaining independence: many peers are independent (crossbenchers) so are less likely to be swayed by party-political considerations.
+ Revising and advising on legislation: the Lords as a whole has a key role in revising and advising on legislation. It is often known as the 'think again' house. Given its lack of any democratic mandate (and the Parliament Act), it cannot block legislation or force its views on government or the Commons.

> **Crossbenchers** Non-party-political peers. In effect, they are independent members of the Lords; an example is the former top civil servant Lord Kerslake.
>
> **Mandate** The authority, given by the electorate, to carry out a policy. A party that wins a large majority of seats in the general election can be said to have a strong mandate from the people.

The Lords and representation

As an unelected chamber, the Lords does not represent voters directly. Many of its members are affiliated to a political party, often being retired or defeated MPs (e.g. Lord Prescott was previously deputy prime minister), so they indirectly fulfil the mandate representation model.

Some peers are chosen on account of their distinction and achievements in particular spheres of public life, such as sport or the arts (e.g. the Paralympian and broadcaster Tanni Grey-Thompson) so, again, indirectly they represent those interests.

The significance of the Commons and the Lords

The work of committees

The work of the various committees is summarised in Table 2.2.

Table 2.2 Committees and their functions, characteristics and significance

Type of committee	Key functions and characteristics	Significance
Public bill committees	+ Go through bills clause by clause, debate and suggest amendments. + Temporary, only meet while a bill is in the committee stage of the legislative process.	+ Ensure bills are properly written and can fulfil the aims of their writers. + An opportunity for other MPs, peers and interest groups to lobby and suggest changes. + Major changes are unlikely as the governing party has a majority on the committee and party whips choose the members on each committee.
Commons select committees	+ Provide a more general oversight of the workings of government departments and ministerial actions. + Less party political and partisan, for example they sit in a horseshoe form rather than as two opposing sides facing each other. Aim for greater cross-party collaboration and consensus. + Many are chaired by opposition backbenchers. + Able to select their own areas for investigation and can summon witnesses.	+ Comprised entirely of backbench MPs. + Committee chairs are elected by their fellow MPs, not selected by party whips. + Produce reports to which the government must usually reply within 60 days. + The government is not obliged to carry out any findings or recommendations in their reports. + Their reports and hearings often generate publicity in the media. + Individuals can refuse to appear. This is truer for foreign nationals such as Facebook's (now Meta) CEO, Mark Zuckerberg, who in 2018 refused for the third time to attend a select committee investigating fake news. British citizens can be compelled to attend or be punished for contempt of parliament.

Check your understanding and progress at www.hoddereducation.co.uk/myrevisionnotesdownloads

Type of committee	Key functions and characteristics	Significance
Lords select committees	+ Investigate specialist subjects, taking advantage of the Lords' expertise and the greater amount of time (compared to MPs) available to them to examine issues. + Currently six main committees, covering: the EU, communications, science and technology, economic affairs, the constitution and international relations.	+ Often contain genuine specialists in their field. + The governing party does not have a majority on the committees.
Public Accounts Committee (Commons only)	+ Traditionally chaired by an experienced opposition backbencher (Meg Hillier in 2022). + Scrutinises value for money in public spending and how well/efficiently the government delivers public services.	+ Covers a wide range of policy areas. Recent reports have ranged from the effectiveness of the NHS Track and Trace system during the pandemic to the cost of policing protests against the HS2 rail project.
Backbench Business Committee (Commons only)	+ Selects topics for debate in parliament on days not given over to government business. Such debates can take place both in the chamber and in Westminster Hall. + Oversees e-petitions.	+ Enables backbenchers to have a greater say in what is debated. + Topics have included the conflict in Yemen and Jobcentre Plus office closures. + Such debates are better at raising issues than generating legislation or government action.
Commons Liaison Committee	+ Comprises all the chairs of the Commons select committees. + Usually chaired by a senior and independent-minded backbencher of the governing party. + Chooses select committee reports for debate in Westminster Hall. + Questions the prime minister on aspects of public policy, usually three times a year.	+ Provides a more measured and focused way for ordinary MPs to make the prime minister accountable, without the theatrics of PMQs. + Co-ordinates the roles of select committees. + Sometimes the prime minister is reluctant to appear. Boris Johnson postponed his appearance twice before cancelling his third scheduled meeting in October 2019. He made his first appearance in May 2020. + Has no ability to force the government or prime minister to change policy. + There was controversy when Sir Bernard Jenkin was chosen by the government directly to be the Commons Liaison Committee chair in 2020, partly as he was not a current select committee chair.

How effective and significant are select committees?

+ Select committees are certainly active and between them produce dozens of reports each year. Among the areas investigated and scrutinised in the 2019–21 parliamentary session was the government's handling of the Covid-19 pandemic and cladding on blocks of flats following the Grenfell Tower tragedy.
+ It is estimated that around 40% of committee recommendations are accepted by the government and a similar proportion go on to be implemented. Around one-third of recommendations for major policy changes succeed. The 2016 report by the Work and Pensions Select Committee into the collapse of the retailer BHS and the loss of much of its employees' pension fund resulted in the company and its owners being reported to the Pensions Regulator.
+ Committee chairs are paid a salary equivalent to that of a junior minister, offering MPs an attractive career alternative to ministerial office.

Party whips MPs in charge of persuading their party's MPs to remain loyal. They seek to do this by argument and sometimes by inducements, such as the prospect of promotion.

Role of the opposition

The opposition's role is to:
+ provide scrutiny and reasoned criticism of government policies and actions in debates and via parliamentary questions
+ suggest amendments to bills
+ argue for alternatives — what they would do if in power
+ provide a 'government-in-waiting', especially with a shadow cabinet
+ nominate the topics for debates on 20 days in each parliamentary session; 17 go to the official opposition party, three to the second-largest opposition party.

Influence of parliament on government decisions

Parliament influences government decisions in the following ways:
+ the committee system and committee reports
+ election of select committee chairs and members (no longer appointed by party whips)
+ debates and questions
+ backbench rebellions in the Commons
+ informal lobbying of ministers by MPs and peers
+ amending legislation, especially in the Lords.

However, there are limits to parliament's influence on government:
+ Governments can and do ignore select committee reports.
+ Select committees are poorly resourced compared to government departments.
+ Government majorities usually see off backbench revolts.
+ Party whips ensure party discipline.
+ The government is in control of most of the parliamentary timetable.
+ Many MPs aspire to promotion so are wary of upsetting the party leadership.
+ The government can use its Commons majority to override the Lords' amendments or rejection of a bill using, if necessary, the Parliament Act.

Party discipline in the Commons

+ Both the governing and opposition parties use a whipping system to enforce party discipline and minimise internal dissent in parliamentary votes.
+ Most governments have large and stable enough majorities to defeat backbench rebellions (e.g. the Blair government and student tuition fees) and thus outvote the opposition.
+ Party discipline is most fragile when a government has only a small or non-existent majority and seeks to get through legislation that is controversial with some of its own backbenchers and the main opposition parties. However, much of the time party discipline does not need to be enforced as MPs will naturally vote the way their leadership wants.
+ The most important votes are termed three-line whips, when MPs must turn up and vote the way their leaders wish.
+ Votes on matters of conscience, such as assisted dying or abortion, are not usually whipped, allowing MPs a free vote.
+ Whips exert further control over party discipline by partly controlling the allocation of MPs to public bill committees, although select committee chairs and membership are now decided by a secret ballot of all MPs, thereby weakening the whips' power.

Three-line whips Parliamentary votes when MPs must follow the voting orders of the whips. Failure to do so by a minister would lead to resignation or dismissal. Backbenchers who frequently rebel are unlikely to be offered posts in the government or on the opposition front bench.

Free vote A vote when MPs are free to vote how they wish, rather than being instructed to vote a certain way by the party leadership.

Check your understanding and progress at www.hoddereducation.co.uk/myrevisionnotesdownloads

Government control of civil servants

+ Traditionally, the government had a lot of control over civil servants appearing before select committees.
+ The original Osmotherly Rules allowed plenty of scope for senior civil servants to be evasive and vague in their answers before committees. However, they were revised in 2014 and civil servants are now required to be as helpful as possible in providing accurate, truthful and full information in accordance with the duties and responsibilities of the Civil Service Code.
+ For example, in 2016 the Home Affairs Select Committee ejected Oliver Robbins, a senior civil servant, for failing to respond adequately to questions about the budget of the UK's border force. Civil servants must balance their answers with due regard to ministerial accountability and not deliberately undermine their political masters — the ministers.

> **Osmotherly Rules**
> Guidance given to civil servants and other government officials appearing before select committees. Various versions of the rules have been in operation since 1980, but they have never been formally accepted by parliament. The rules were most recently updated in October 2014.

Now test yourself
TESTED

12 In the Lords, what is a crossbench peer?
13 Must the government adopt the recommendations of the parliamentary select committee?
14 Before which select committee does the prime minister appear?
15 What is a three-line whip?

Answers on p. 124

How parliament interacts with other branches of government

Key points
REVISED

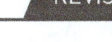

+ Parliament provides the personnel for government: prime minister and ministers.
+ It is the forum where government is primarily called to account and scrutinised.
+ It passes the laws that are then interpreted and enforced by the judiciary.
+ Any laws passed must be compatible with international agreements such as the European Convention on Human Rights (ECHR).

Summary

You should now have an understanding of:
+ the key features of parliament
+ how parliament checks the executive
+ the main stages of the legislative process
+ the different theories of representation
+ the powers and importance of MPs and peers
+ how MPs and peers can influence governments
+ how committees function in parliament
+ the extent to which parliament as a body can influence government decisions
+ how party discipline is enforced
+ how parliament relates to other branches of government.

> **Exam skills**
>
> Consider the following Section C essay title:
>
> 1 'The greatest power of backbench MPs is voting on legislation.' Analyse and evaluate this statement.
>
> For the Section C questions, you need to break down the answer into relevant themes and analyse and evaluate each one in turn. Identifying key themes is therefore crucial to writing an effective answer. Do not worry if you have more themes than can be analysed in 40 minutes — select three or four of the most obvious ones. It is better to analyse a few in some depth than to cover a large number superficially. Some suggested themes for this essay title are provided below:
>
> + The power of voting on legislation. Clearly important, as law-making is a major power and role, but also severely limited by the whipping system. Mention though the power that backbench rebellions can sometimes have.
> + Sitting on committees. Mention both public bill and select committees, and comment on how backbenchers are far more likely to be independent and critical of their own party in select committees, but that their power is muted by the relative impotence of these committees in forcing the hand of government.
> + Dealing with constituents' problems. Explain about surgeries and the political incentive to be seen to be representing their voters/redress grievances, but also be aware that MPs can never really force local authorities/bodies to change policy.
> + Removal of the prime minister. Occasionally backbenchers from the ruling party can weaken/remove the prime minister, for example Thatcher directly and May indirectly.

> **Exam practice**
>
> 1 Explain and analyse three stages in the parliamentary legislative process. [9]
> 2 Read the following extract.
>
> > Select committee members build up worthwhile expertise in that area and a more effective 'corporate' spirit than in the past. Attendance at committee sessions has increased and there is more of a premium on effective engagement by members. Select committee chairs attract a good deal of media attention. It increasingly attracts serious ex-ministers and genuinely expert and less-partisan backbenchers, who can command regular engagement from their committee members.
> >
> > Both departmental and bill committees mostly operate by calling 'witnesses' to give evidence and taking written evidence from relevant or involved bodies. This is a weak and old-fashioned form of information gathering. It produces a lot of arguments that committees do not have the staff or expertise to critically or objectively assess — except in a vague and rather general manner. Select committees' powers to compel witnesses to appear and to tell the truth seem weak and undefined. Senior civil servants have to appear before select committees, but ministers may refuse. The committees can invite outsiders to appear, and they might be in contempt of parliament if they fail to show up. Witnesses have to answer questions but can claim not to know or have information with impunity.
> >
> > Source: adapted from a 2018 study by Democratic Audit, an independent research unit based at the LSE
>
> Analyse, evaluate and compare the arguments in the extract above for and against the view that select committees are effective in scrutinising governments. [25]
>
> **Answers available online**

3 The prime minister and cabinet

Key points

+ The prime minister and their cabinet constitute the government or executive of the UK. They are the main source of policy making and parliamentary legislation.
+ Although prime ministers enjoy considerable freedom, such as their ability to choose ministers, they can also be vulnerable, especially if they only have a small Commons majority or are faring badly in the polls.
+ All members of the government (and especially the cabinet) must, in public at least, display loyalty to the prime minister and defend all aspects of government policy.
+ Many of the powers of the prime minister tend to be variable, not least according to the prevailing political climate.

The prime minister

Main functions and role

The prime minister is the head of the executive (government), chair of the cabinet and in charge of the civil service. The role includes:

+ leading the government, with overall responsibility for both domestic and foreign policy
+ selecting the cabinet and all junior government posts
+ being the dominant figure in the core executive
+ representing the country abroad; attending international gatherings of world leaders, e.g. G7 summits; and hosting UK-based international gatherings, such as the 2021 Glasgow COP26 conference on climate change
+ being the party leader
+ being the main 'defender and explainer' of government policy and actions in both parliament and the media
+ chairing cabinet meetings
+ heading up the civil service
+ being the monarch's first minister and *primus inter pares* with other ministers.

> **Core executive** The collective term for the key players in government policy making. It comprises the prime minister, the cabinet and its various committees, the Cabinet Office and senior civil servants.
>
> **Primus inter pares** The traditional notion that the prime minister is merely the 'first among equals' among fellow members of the cabinet. In reality, modern prime ministers have far more power.

Exam tips

Be careful to distinguish between the terms 'executive' (prime minister and cabinet) and 'core executive' (prime minister, cabinet and its various committees, Cabinet Office and senior civil servants). The core executive is a more wide-ranging term and usefully suggests how power is spread beyond the immediate circle of ministers and prime minister.

If discussing the power of the prime minister to reshuffle their cabinet, try to use the most recent example available. Boris Johnson carried out his third reshuffle in early 2022 when, among other changes, Jacob Rees-Mogg took on a new role as minister for Brexit opportunities.

Main powers and resources

REVISED

The prime minister's main powers and resources include:
- prerogative powers (the royal prerogative)
- shaping and deciding policy, both nationally and for England
- de facto commander-in-chief of the armed forces
- patronage — choosing their cabinet and promoting, demoting and reshuffling members as appropriate
- arranging the structure of cabinet committees and often chairing many committees
- high media profile — plenty of opportunities to explain and defend government actions to the public and to parliament
- as leader of the largest party in the Commons, they are normally able to command a working majority to get their legislative plans through, which gives them a lot of control over parliamentary business
- able to make use of the civil service (especially the Cabinet Office) and special advisers (SpAds) for policy input and advice
- usually able to claim authority or a mandate from the people by winning the general election; prime ministers who assume office mid-term, such as Gordon Brown in 2007, are often said to be weakened by the lack of a direct mandate.

> **Exam tip**
>
> When analysing the power of the prime minister to decide policy, mention how this is a more significant power in England since devolution. Much domestic policy, e.g. health and education, are nowadays decided by the regional assemblies.

> **Exam tips**
>
> The power of commander-in-chief does not mean the prime minister personally leads the armed forces into battle, but rather that they can deploy them as necessary. In reality, however, most major military operations are preceded by a parliamentary debate and vote.
>
> Do not confuse politically neutral civil servants, who are permanent and 'inherited' by a prime minister, with special advisers, such as Boris Johnson's former adviser Dominic Cummings, who are temporary and personally appointed by the prime minister to provide political advice.

> **Revision activity**
>
> Create a spider diagram of the prime ministerial powers to show the relative importance of each power, e.g. by using different colours or size of text.

The cabinet

Key points

REVISED

- The cabinet is the team of just over 20 senior government ministers and other key officials, such as the chief whip, who are directly appointed by the prime minister. They normally meet once a week on Thursday mornings. These meetings are chaired by the prime minister, who also largely determines the agenda.
- Much of its detailed work is done in cabinet committees.
- Most members are MPs, although there are normally a couple of peers present as well, including the leader of the House of Lords.

- Prime ministers often reshuffle the cabinet in order to bring in new talent or 'freshen up' their team, to sack underperforming ministers or to fill gaps caused by death or resignation.
- The cabinet's proceedings are kept secret and all members publicly support its decisions. This principle is known as collective cabinet responsibility. Different prime ministers have managed the cabinet in different ways, reflecting their own style and personality.
- The cabinet is seen as the traditional basis for policy making in the UK. However, many have argued that, in reality, prime ministers rather than the cabinet as a whole dominate decision making, hence Lord Hailsham's famous 1976 reference to an 'elective dictatorship'.
- Formal votes on policy and decisions are rare; prime ministers usually aim for agreement by consensus. However, it was reported in May 2018 that the Brexit 'war cabinet' subcommittee rejected the prime minister's plan for a customs partnership with the EU by a vote of 6 to 5 against.

The cabinet is sometimes characterised by informal smaller groupings such as the inner cabinet (or 'kitchen cabinet') comprising just a handful of senior cabinet ministers. Some prime ministers, such as Tony Blair, preferred even smaller meetings, known as 'sofa government', often with individual ministers. These are sometimes regarded as undermining proper cabinet government.

Cabinet committees

REVISED

- Cabinet committees are groups of ministers that take collective decisions, many of them routine. They can also include subcommittees.
- The composition, membership and terms of reference are decided solely by the prime minister.
- They tend to comprise ministers from several related departments to enable joined-up government, e.g. the Social Reform Committee includes the secretaries of state for education, health and social care as well as work and pensions.
- Their decisions are as binding on the rest of the cabinet as those made by the full cabinet.
- There was a significant reduction to five main committees in 2017, with four of them chaired by the prime minister.

Some examples of cabinet committees are given in Table 3.1.

Table 3.1 Examples of cabinet committees in 2021

Committee	Functions/remit
National Security Council	The main forum for discussion and consideration of government objectives for national security. Looks strategically at the issue. Not the same as the emergency council known as Cobra.
European Union Exit and Trade Committee	Oversees the UK's exit negotiations with the EU.
Covid-19 Strategy Committee	Oversees the government's response to the pandemic, and plots the direction for the recovery strategy.

Reshuffle When ministers are moved around government departments; some will be promoted, some moved sideways and some sacked from government altogether. The most infamous reshuffle was carried out by Harold Macmillan in 1962 when he sacked seven cabinet colleagues, known as the 'Night of the Long Knives'.

Collective cabinet responsibility The principle whereby all members of the cabinet support its decisions in public, even if they disagree with them in private and argued against them in cabinet discussion. It is seen as vital to the effective functioning of cabinet government.

Inner cabinet A smaller, more informal group of senior ministers who meet outside of regular sessions of the full cabinet. It is often seen as the place where the real decisions are made.

Joined-up government A policy to make different departments in the same government work together.

How policy is made

Key players

REVISED

All the key players listed in Table 3.2 play a role in policy making. Different policies will involve the key players to a varying extent.

Table 3.2 Key players in the policy-making process

Key player	Examples in practice	Significance
Prime minister	+ Most prime ministers enter No 10 with a clear policy agenda often based on personal convictions and principles, e.g. Boris Johnson and 'Getting Brexit done'. + They often have a catchy strapline, such as David Cameron's 'Big Society'.	+ Very important. Prime ministers seek to prioritise their key policies so as to make their mark and leave behind a tangible legacy. + A working majority in the Commons means they can normally ensure such legislation gets through, although prime ministers with small or non-existent majorities have a harder time. Those in coalition government have to negotiate policy with the junior coalition party.
The cabinet	+ Will normally discuss and debate policy initiatives and 'rubber stamp' them. + Where there are disagreements, such as over spending priorities, these are often resolved at cabinet meetings.	+ Often considerable, especially if the party is divided, a policy is controversial and/or the prime minister is seen as relatively weak. + Much of the finer detail for the Brexit negotiations from 2017 onwards was thrashed out in the cabinet.
Senior civil servants	+ Can offer advice and guidance to government ministers. Crucial in the actual delivery of policy, e.g. the 2012 London Olympics and the National Citizen Service. + Influence ministers by 'speaking truth unto power'. + In early 2022, the Head of the Civil Service and Cabinet Secretary was Simon Case.	+ As permanent and non-party political, their advice should be unbiased and objective. + Should not offer advice about the rights or wrongs of a particular policy but advise on implementation, legality, cost implications and other practicalities. + Provide long experience of government and handling different issues and policies across the political spectrum. + Increasingly share responsibility for providing policy advice with special advisers.
Special advisers (SpAds)	+ Party-political figures hand-picked by the prime minister. + Temporary civil servants; unlike permanent civil servants, not required to offer balanced advice. + Normally replaced by an incoming prime minister, even one from the same party. + There were 113 advisers in March 2021 (compared to around 420,000 civil servants).	+ Have assumed increasing prominence and notoriety in recent years, e.g. Alastair Campbell (Tony Blair) and Dominic Cummings (Boris Johnson). + Frequently seen to 'have the ear of the prime minister' and to have played a major part in policy formation, e.g. much of the Johnson government's hard-line approach to Brexit was due to the influence of Dominic Cummings. + They can also prove controversial figures. Cummings, for example, faced much criticism for breaking Covid-19 travel rules by travelling to Barnard Castle in Durham. He was later sacked, but his subsequent harsh criticism of the government caused significant embarrassment for Johnson.

Manifesto pledges

REVISED

+ Manifesto pledges are perhaps the easiest to decide upon as the party in power will have agreed these already. 'Get Brexit Done' was a clear and simple slogan that helped the Conservatives win the 2019 election.

Check your understanding and progress at www.hoddereducation.co.uk/myrevisionnotesdownloads

+ It is more complicated for minority/coalition governments, however, that have to make a deal with other parties after the general election. For example, after the inconclusive 2017 election, Prime Minister Theresa May struck a deal with the pro-Brexit and socially conservative Democratic Unionist Party (DUP).

> **Exam tip**
>
> The DUP were not in a formal coalition with the Conservatives between 2017 and 2019 as the Liberal Democrats were from 2010 to 2015. Therefore, they had no ministers in government and only agreed to support the government in crucial votes of confidence (to prevent a no confidence vote in the Commons from ending the government) and supply (it 'supplied' the government with funds by voting for the government's budget). The formal name for this arrangement is a confidence and supply deal.

Collaboration

REVISED

+ Many policy decisions and strategies require consultation and co-operation between different ministers and government departments (e.g. Brexit). Although the prime minister has the final say on policy, in effect they are often constrained by political reality such as backbench rebellions and the threat of ministerial resignations.
+ Prime ministers who are not very collaborative in policy making, such as Margaret Thatcher and Tony Blair, can find themselves dangerously isolated and vulnerable.
+ Some policy is the result of unforeseen events or emergencies. This applies, for example, to responses (and restrictions) following terrorist attacks such as the 7/7 London bombings and, more recently, the Covid-19 pandemic.

The relationship between prime minister and cabinet

Key points

REVISED

+ In theory, the relationship should be harmonious and fruitful because:
  + the cabinet is selected purely by the prime minister and requires no approval from parliament (unlike in the USA where Senate ratification is required)
  + the prime minister and the cabinet are (usually) from the same political party, coalition government being the exception.
+ In reality, however, most prime ministers experience fractious relations with the cabinet some of the time due to a number of factors:
  + Political parties are broad-based so contain a variety of views and, therefore, factions emerge, such as Brexiteers and Remainers under Theresa May. Prime ministers need to include all the main strands of party opinion in their cabinet to keep their party relatively united.
  + Most cabinets contain 'big beasts', politicians who are too senior or popular to leave out, e.g. Boris Johnson in Theresa May's cabinet until he resigned in July 2018 over the prime minister's Brexit deal proposals.
  + As cabinets contain some of the brightest and best MPs, they also include many individuals with high ambitions and/or big egos. Any cabinet contains a mixture of foes, rivals and allies.
  + Factions often gather around strong individuals, e.g. Blairites and Brownites.
  + Each minister is lobbying for departmental resources and wants priority given to their department's financial demands, whether it is more money for the NHS or the latest military equipment.

> **Brexiteers** Those who supported the Leave campaign in the 2016 EU referendum.
>
> **Remainers** Those who supported the Remain campaign in the 2016 EU referendum.
>
> **Blairites** Labour MPs regarded as being loyal to Prime Minister Tony Blair during the Labour governments of 1997–2010. Peter Mandelson was a prominent member of this group.
>
> **Brownites** Labour MPs regarded as being loyal to Chancellor Gordon Brown during the Labour governments of 1997–2010. Ed Balls was a prominent member of this group.

The difference between individual and collective responsibility

Individual (ministerial) responsibility

REVISED

- The notion that each minister is personally responsible for the actions and outcomes in their department.
- Involves answering questions in the Commons and in the media on behalf of their department.
- In theory, mistakes and policy failures in a department could lead to a minister resigning. In practice, this is rare and ministers tend to resign for other reasons.
- Less significant nowadays as ministers often devolve blame for policy failures to civil servants or heads of executive agencies. For example, in 2020 it was the chief civil servant at the Department for Education, Jonathan Slater, who was sacked following the row over the awarding of GCSE and A-level grades that summer. Education Secretary Gavin Williamson stayed in post until removed in a cabinet reshuffle in September 2021.
- Ministers whose personal conduct falls below that expected of someone in public life and/or breaches the Ministerial Code would be expected to resign or face dismissal by the prime minister. This is often linked to personal scandal. The Ministerial Code was first issued in 2010. Key principles include:
  - avoiding any conflict of interest between private interests and public duties
  - not accepting any gifts or offers of hospitality that could be construed as bribery or attempting to influence decisions
  - upholding the principle of civil service impartiality
  - abiding by the principles of collective cabinet responsibility
  - not meeting foreign dignitaries or politicians without the prime minister's permission and without civil servants present.

On occasion, even the prime minister has been accused of breaching the Ministerial Code. This accusation was levelled against Boris Johnson in 2021 over an anonymous donation of £60,000 to help fund refurbishment of the prime minister's private Downing Street flat.

> **Case study**
>
> **Dismissal for breaching the Ministerial Code**
>
> Priti Patel was forced to resign as international development secretary by Theresa May in November 2017 for not being open and honest about secret meetings with Israeli ministers and businesspeople while on a private holiday in Israel.
>
> Not only did Priti Patel break the Ministerial Code by meeting senior Israeli officials without the knowledge of the prime minister and the Foreign Office, it also emerged that she had been less than completely truthful with Theresa May when the story first appeared.

Collective cabinet responsibility

REVISED

- The convention that all ministers, and not just those in the cabinet, are bound by government policies and must defend and promote them in public.
- A minister who cannot in good conscience agree with government policy should resign.

+ Occasionally, collective cabinet responsibility is suspended by the prime minister when there are clear and open divisions within the cabinet. This is principally true of EU membership. Both Harold Wilson (Labour prime minister 1964–70 and 1974–6) and David Cameron formally suspended it before referendums on continued membership of the EEC/EU.
+ Free votes, such as those on issues of conscience, are also not normally bound by the convention.
+ Occasionally, ministers can publicly breach collective cabinet responsibility and survive. For example, Ken Clarke and Theresa May made conflicting statements about the future of the Human Rights Act in 2010–11.
+ Some ministers secretly breach collective cabinet responsibility by speaking to journalists off the record or by leaking documents to the press.
+ In January 2018, Boris Johnson was criticised for revealing in advance that he would argue at cabinet for £5 billion extra to be spent on the NHS.
+ It enables the prime minister and government to present a strong and united front to the media, the public and their backbenchers.

Off the record When a minister or other politician speaks to a journalist on the condition of complete anonymity. Therefore, a story will refer vaguely to 'sources close to the prime minister' and not mention a name.

Making links

Collective cabinet responsibility is a good example of a constitutional convention. Conventions are explained in Chapter 1.

Now test yourself
TESTED

1 How often does the cabinet normally meet?
2 Who appoints, removes and reshuffles the cabinet?
3 How many full cabinet committees were there in 2018 under Theresa May?
4 When was the Ministerial Code first introduced?
5 Which prime minister suspended collective cabinet responsibility over continued membership of the European Economic Community (EEC)?
6 Name one minister who breached collective cabinet responsibility but survived.
7 Which cabinet minister had to resign because they met members of a foreign government without civil servants present on a private trip abroad?
8 What was the major divide within Theresa May's cabinet after the 2017 election?
9 Who do ministers often blame for operational failures in their departments?
10 What does *primus inter pares* mean?

Answers on p. 124

Resignations
REVISED

Table 3.3 outlines two resignations owing to individual and collective cabinet/ministerial responsibility.

Table 3.3 Examples of resignations

Example	Cause of resignation	Details and background
Sir Thomas Dugdale's 1954 resignation as Minister of Agriculture	Individual (ministerial) responsibility	+ An official inquiry found serious flaws in procedures and practices by civil servants regarding a case of compulsory purchase of farmland for a military airfield. + Dugdale resigned although he had nothing to do with the original decisions. + He resigned because he accepted full responsibility for the actions of officials in his department.
Iain Duncan Smith's 2016 resignation as work and pensions secretary	Collective ministerial responsibility	+ Duncan Smith left David Cameron's cabinet over planned cuts to disability benefits, which he described as 'a compromise too far'. + He felt unable on principle to support such a policy.

Other examples of government resignations over policy difference include Robin Cook in 2003 over the Iraq War, and Caroline Ansell in 2020 over funding of free school meals during the holidays.

Why else do ministers resign or lose office?

+ Removed via a cabinet reshuffle to make way for fresh faces.
+ Seen as underperforming, for example being a poor media or Commons performer.
+ Ill health: James Brokenshire resigned from the cabinet as Northern Ireland secretary to undergo cancer treatment in January 2018. He returned to government later that year, but again resigned as security minister in 2021 to undergo further medical treatment. He died later that year.
+ Personal scandal: easily the most common cause. This usually involves financial misconduct (such as expenses), e.g. Maria Miller as culture secretary in 2014, or other misconduct, e.g. health secretary Matt Hancock in 2021, who broke rules on social distancing while conducting a secret affair. In such cases, the tipping point is normally when they lose the prime minister's confidence and become a distraction to the overall work of the government. The case of Hancock was exacerbated by his antics being caught on a hidden camera and then widely circulated by the media.

> **Exam tip**
>
> Do not include policy failure as a common cause of ministerial resignation. Most major policy initiatives are decided by the whole cabinet and the prime minister. Policy implementation is also not a frequent cause for resignation nowadays. Ministers are much more willing to blame senior civil servants or executive agency chiefs when things go wrong.

> **Revision activity**
>
> Research and make bullet point notes on the following:
> + three ministers who have resigned due to personal scandal since 2010
> + three ministers who been removed in cabinet reshuffles since 2010
> + three ministers who have been promoted in cabinet reshuffles since 2010.
>
> Include the name, date, post and a brief explanation.

> **Now test yourself** TESTED
>
> 11 Read the scenarios below and decide which category of resignation is correct, selecting from:
>   a individual ministerial responsibility
>   b collective cabinet responsibility
>   c loss of confidence by the prime minister
>   d personal scandal
>
> | Scenario | Category |
> | --- | --- |
> | A tabloid newspaper reports on a minister persuading his wife to lie to the police so he avoids getting speeding points on his driving licence. | |
> | A minister resigns because of swingeing cuts to their departmental budget. | |
> | The prime minister is facing mounting calls from the media and even some backbench MPs to sack a minister who is alleged to have made anti-Semitic remarks at a private dinner. | |
> | A minister resigns after their department is heavily criticised for failing to handle asylum requests quickly and fairly. | |
>
> Answers on p. 124

The power to determine policy making

Introduction of the poll tax, 1990

Background/motives

- A longstanding Conservative policy to reform local government taxation and end domestic rates, and a 1987 manifesto pledge.
- Many Conservatives wanted to rein in high-spending Labour councils, many of whose voters did not pay rates.
- A desire to spread the cost of local government services, such as education and social care, more fairly. Domestic rates taxed homes regardless of the number of residents (and their use of local services) or their income. They also were not directly payable by tenants.
- The poll tax (the official name was the community charge) was a flat rate tax payable by nearly all adults.
- The policy was strongly supported by Margaret Thatcher herself. She personally annotated many of the briefings and memorandums about the proposals.
- First trialled in Scotland, where it had proved unpopular and difficult to implement.
- Although undefeated after three general elections and with a decent Commons majority, Thatcher was facing increasing criticism for her dictatorial style and unwillingness to listen to critics within her own party and even the cabinet.

Outcome

- Aroused strong hostility on the left; many refused to pay the new tax.
- Mass protests, including a number of violent tax riots involving tens of thousands of protestors.
- Opposition was especially strong in staunchly Labour areas such as South Yorkshire, already alienated by the 1984–5 miners' strike and pit closures.
- Many of Thatcher's MPs disliked the policy and criticised the prime minister. The growing opposition from Tory MPs and supporters played a major part in a formal leadership challenge from ex-minister Michael Heseltine in November 1990. Thatcher failed to secure enough votes in the first ballot and subsequently resigned as prime minister and Tory leader soon afterwards.
- The policy was scrapped soon after Thatcher's resignation and replaced by the council tax in 1993.

Measures dealing with the Covid-19 pandemic, 2020–1

Background/motives

- The onset of the global pandemic in early 2020 brought huge and unprecedented challenges for both the nation and Johnson's government in terms of the economy and the impact on the NHS and individual lives.
- Government policy was very much determined by pragmatism and events, i.e. what worked/didn't work, as it was nearly impossible to plan and enact policy in the rapidly changing situation.
- There was a lot of criticism early on concerning issues such as the supply of personal protective equipment (PPE) to frontline health workers, the 'track and trace' system and the awarding of some contracts to friends and political allies of the prime minister and ministers: 'Covid cronyism'.

- The government was forced to borrow billions of pounds to fund the costs of the furlough scheme for workers laid off temporarily, emergency loans to the worst-affected businesses and temporary increases in benefits such as Universal Credit. There was also the added strain and costs on the NHS due to hospitalisations and the vaccine roll-out programme.
- The prime minister could only dictate policy, e.g. lockdowns, in England; the devolved assemblies followed their own policies, often more cautious. This led to variations in rules across the UK. For example, face masks in public spaces remained obligatory longer in Wales compared to England.
- Policy making was heavily influenced by medical experts, e.g. members of the SAGE (Scientific Advisory Group for Emergencies) committee; at public briefings, many of the questions were handled by scientists such as Professor Chris Whitty rather than by politicians.
- Opposition parties had to be careful in their approach, as they could not oppose all government policy on principle. Many measures, such as the national lockdown, were universally agreed to be necessary based on scientific data and policies in other nations. Labour, therefore, largely went along with the key measures, and instead focused on criticising policy implementation and allegations of corruption and mixed messaging by government ministers.

Outcome

- Government handling of the crisis was extremely mixed. Some early stages, such as the track and trace system operated by private companies including Serco, were considered shambolic, suggesting a lack of preparation. Later stages, such as the rapid vaccine roll-out, proved much more successful, with the result that most legal restrictions such as banning large-scale gatherings and compulsory face-mask wearing could be lifted by summer 2021. Restrictions were partially reintroduced in late 2021 due to the spread of the Omicron variant, but relaxed again in early 2022, demonstrating how policy can quickly alter in times of crisis.
- Some of the most damning criticisms on the prime minister's handling of the crisis came from disgraced special adviser Dominic Cummings. In one statement before a parliamentary inquiry in May 2021, he commented: 'I would say, if you took anybody at random from the top 1% of competent people in country and presented them with the situation, they would have behaved differently to how the prime minister behaved.' Cummings had himself been earlier accused of breaking lockdown rules.
- The crisis proved to have mixed political fortunes for the Tory Party. On one hand, in the midst of the pandemic they won the Hartlepool by-election, winning the seat off Labour, and fared well in the May 2021 local elections. On the other hand, in June 2021 they went on to lose Chesham and Amersham, a safe Buckinghamshire seat, to the Liberal Democrats.
- Allegations that the PM allowed and attended some parties at No 10, dubbed 'Partygate' by the media, led to a drop in Conservative support at the polls by the start of 2022. There were demands for his resignation from some Conservative backbenchers.
- The huge financial costs will affect fiscal policy for years to come.
- This was very much a global crisis, and the mixed pattern of successes/failures could be seen in most other developed countries.
- The pandemic was a classic example of policy being determined primarily by events and non-political experts, rather than by the prime minister and ministers.

> **Making links**
>
> Both these policy decisions could be compared with the fundamental values of the Conservatives. Arguably, the poll tax fitted in better with Thatcherite conservatism than did the management of the Covid-19 pandemic. Many Conservative MPs were wary of the infringements on individual liberty required by the national lockdowns and subsequent restrictions on businesses such as hospitality. The huge borrowing required also marked a major break from the more prudent, low-tax policy favoured by most Tories.

Comparing these events

REVISED

Table 3.4 highlights some of the similarities and differences between Thatcher's introduction of the poll tax and Johnson's management of the Covid-19 pandemic.

Table 3.4 Similarities and differences between these events

Similarities	Differences
<ul><li>Both were very damaging to the prime minister of the time and seen as major blots on their reputations.</li><li>There was a strong personal commitment to the policy by the prime minister, who took the leading role in defending and explaining their policies.</li><li>Seen as examples of the prime minister not taking criticism seriously or listening to advice that did not accord with their own views.</li><li>Aroused criticism within their own parties.</li><li>Both were formally voted upon and approved by parliament.</li></ul>	<ul><li>While the early stages of managing the pandemic went badly for Johnson, his government received credit later on during the crisis for the swift roll-out of the vaccination programme, which he saw as the main route out of the crisis.</li><li>With the global pandemic, Johnson was often accused of not really leading on policy and delegating too much. Also, he was accused of sending out mixed and sometimes confused messaging.</li><li>One was a clear manifesto pledge, whereas the other was about responding rapidly to unexpected and unprecedented global events.</li><li>Criticism of Johnson's handling of the pandemic was more muted among his backbenchers. His harshest critic was his former SpAd.</li><li>The global pandemic was arguably more damaging given the loss of life and financial cost.</li></ul>

Relations between government and parliament

Theory

REVISED

The government should be checked by and answerable to parliament. Ministers should be personally accountable to parliament, e.g. via oral questions. Governments should be able to get their business through Westminster easily due to a working majority, the power of the party whips and the limited power of the Lords.

Reality

REVISED

Governments often avoid effective scrutiny in the main chamber due to party loyalties and the theatrical or ritualistic nature of questions, especially PMQs. The most effective scrutiny of government arguably comes via select committees or bodies such as the National Audit Office (NAO). The NAO, for example, produced a report in 2021 on the Crossrail project that identified a shortfall in funding of between £30 million and £218 million.

Ministers rarely take personal responsibility for failings in their departments. Ministers most commonly resign due to personal scandals rather than policy differences (inability to accept collective cabinet responsibility) or ministerial accountability.

The growing willingness of backbenchers to rebel means that government policies do not always have a smooth ride through the Commons. This is especially true if their majority is small or the prime minister is already facing a high level of criticism from within their own party.

> **National Audit Office (NAO)** An independent government body responsible for scrutinising the use of public money and ensuring it is spent efficiently and appropriately. It is essentially the government's spending watchdog.

> **Revision activity**
> Create a list of pros and cons to explain why an MP might rebel against their party leadership.

Now test yourself

TESTED

The following questions concern the policy-making examples given earlier in this chapter: the introduction of the poll tax in 1990 and the handling of the Covid-19 pandemic.

12 Which of these was a manifesto pledge?
13 Which of these two events saw the fiercest criticism come from a former SpAd?
14 What were the main criticisms made of the prime minister in each example?

Answers on p. 124

Summary

You should now have an understanding of:
+ the key powers of the prime minister
+ the composition and function of the cabinet
+ the role and importance of cabinet committees
+ how government policy is made
+ the importance of the prime minister in policy making (via two case studies, one before 1997 and one after)
+ the difference between individual and collective responsibility
+ reasons why ministers might resign
+ the relationship between government and parliament.

Exam skills

In Section B, you will need to look at the provenance of one or two extracts as part of your answer. Imagine if there was a question on prime ministerial leadership with one extract from Tony Blair's memoirs, published in 2010, and the other from a 2019 *Daily Mail* article written during the height of May's Brexit crisis. What is creditworthy about the style and format of the following analysis?

In terms of provenance, Blair's memoirs will obviously provide an informed insider's view but, being memoirs, may well reflect a defensive position and a desire to defend his historical legacy by explaining away mistakes as down to others' actions. The Daily Mail article and its criticism of May's lack of leadership also needs to be treated cautiously. Although a very pro-Conservative paper, the Daily Mail was also very Eurosceptic and therefore critical of May, who was seen as 'soft' on the issue. Also, both extracts were written before the global pandemic, which raised new challenges of leadership.

This evaluation of provenance of both extracts works well as both are seen to be partisan rather than neutral extracts, with a potential axe to grind, though a positive for each extract is also identified. There is also a brief and relevant discussion regarding date. While it is important to include discussion of provenance, it should not be too long and should come right at the start of your answer.

Exam practice

1 Explain and analyse three key aspects of cabinet committees. [9]
2 'The personal involvement of the prime minister is the most dominant factor in the making of policy.' Analyse and evaluate this statement with reference to any two examples (one pre- and one post-1997) that you have studied. [25]

Answers available online

4 The judiciary

Key points

REVISED

+ The judiciary is concerned with applying the law and ensuring that government and other public institutions such as local councils follow their own rules.
+ The judiciary also has a crucial role in protecting citizens' rights.
+ The UK judiciary is organised hierarchically.
+ The UK does not have a unified legal system and there are differences between England and Wales, and Scotland and Northern Ireland.
+ The UK Supreme Court (UKSC) is the only judicial institution that has authority in all parts of the UK.

UK Supreme Court (UKSC) The highest court of appeal in the UK. It has the power to make judgments based on the European Convention on Human Rights (ECHR).

Organisation and key principles

Organisation

REVISED

The judiciary in England and Wales forms a strict hierarchy of importance (Figure 4.1). For example, judges of the Court of Appeal are generally given more weight than district judges sitting in county courts and magistrates' courts.

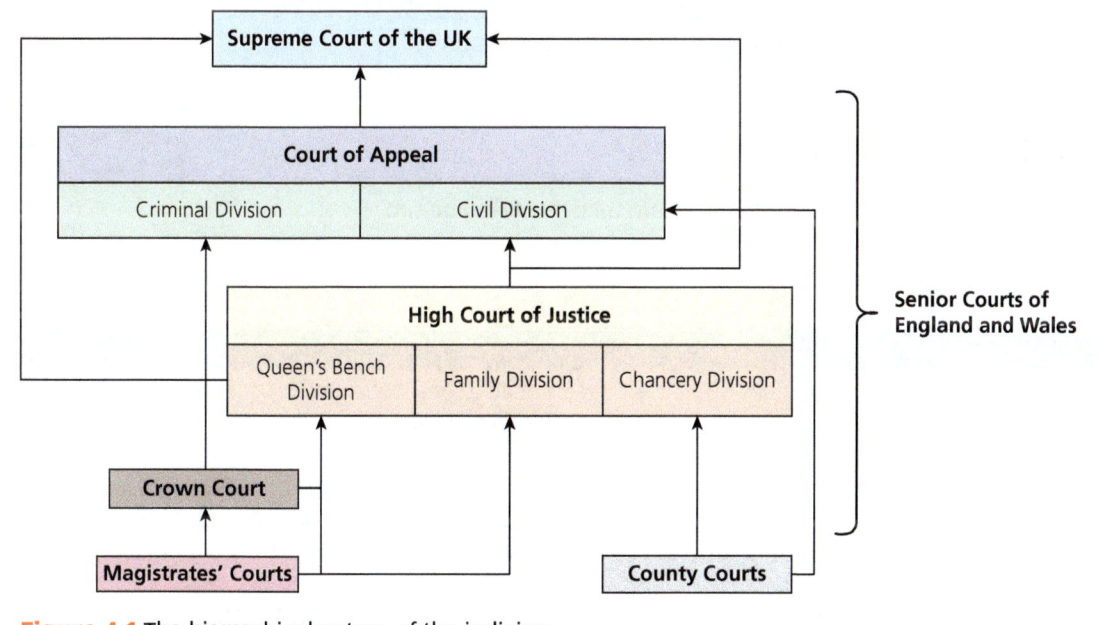

Figure 4.1 The hierarchical nature of the judiciary

Key principles

REVISED

In order to understand the function and powers of the judiciary properly, you need to know some of the key ideas that underpin it.

Judicial independence and impartiality

+ Judicial independence is the notion that judges are free from government interference (i.e. they are independent).
+ This is largely maintained via an independent appointments process and permanent job security for judges. Salaries are set by an independent body, not the government.

Exam tip

There is no need to learn the functions of all the different courts, but you should be aware of the hierarchical nature of them and how each level can overrule those below it.

My Revision Notes AQA A-level UK Politics Second Edition

+ Judicial impartiality or neutrality is the notion that judges are neutral/objective when it comes to making their judgments and are not swayed by personal opinion or popular pressure. This is ensured by professional training and the requirements that UKSC judges must have considerable legal experience. However, the background of many judges is seen by some as unbalanced and thus harmful to true neutrality.

Separation of powers

The judiciary is separate, both physically and in terms of personnel, from parliament and the government. This is seen as crucial to judicial independence and upholding the rule of law.

Ultra vires

This means that everyone is subject to the law of the land, including the government. If governments or other public bodies are deemed by the courts to have exceeded their powers, their actions are declared *ultra vires*, i.e. beyond the power of the law and therefore illegal, and must be reversed. Such decisions are often made after the process of judicial review.

Judicial review

A judicial review is a court proceeding in which judges review the legality of a decision or action made by a public body including the government. Any challenge is to *the way* in which a decision has been made, i.e. about processes, not the rights and wrongs of the conclusion reached.

> **Exam tip**
>
> Make sure you are clear about the difference between judicial independence and judicial impartiality/neutrality. Although similar, they are not the same thing.

> **Exam tip**
>
> Do not confuse a judicial review in the UK with the American process, where courts can declare an action or law unconstitutional and 'strike it down'. No British courts have this power.

Is the judiciary too powerful?

REVISED

Table 4.1 discusses whether the judiciary in the UK could be deemed to be too powerful.

Table 4.1 Is the judiciary in the UK too powerful?

Yes	No
+ Judges, unlike MPs, are unelected and cannot be removed easily. + The Human Rights Act 1998 means judges get involved in politics and often clash with the government, undermining both parliamentary sovereignty and democracy. + Judges make decisions that can have a huge impact, including over life and death (e.g. cases involving assisted dying or switching off life-support machines). + Judicial review means that judges can end up forcing government departments and public bodies to change their policies.	+ Judges need to be independent of politicians in order to be impartial and fair to everyone. + Judges only interpret laws passed by parliament. Parliament has chosen to sign up to the European Convention on Human Rights (ECHR) and to pass the Human Rights Act 1998, and could equally opt to reverse both actions. + Judges are very experienced legal professionals who are properly trained in looking at complex and difficult cases impartially. They are better suited than politicians who might be swayed by public opinion and the media. + The courts make sure that those in power stick to the rules themselves. This is a necessary check to avoid arbitrary government. No one is above the law, even ministers, police and the armed forces.

Check your understanding and progress at www.hoddereducation.co.uk/myrevisionnotesdownloads

Composition and appointment of the judiciary

Appointment procedure

REVISED

+ Judges' appointments are based on merit and experience.
+ Politicians have no real say in judicial appointments, unlike in the USA.
+ Since 2006, all judges below the level of the Supreme Court have been appointed by the independent Judicial Appointments Commission (JAC) via an open and competitive application process. Before then, the lord chancellor had a role in the process. Nowadays, they have only a limited power of veto over JAC appointees.
+ Many have criticised the UK judiciary regarding its composition in terms of gender, race and educational/social background. The judiciary, especially at the most senior levels, has been accused of being 'too privileged, pale and male'.

> **Lord chancellor** The government's senior minister in charge of the law and justice, and a political appointment. Until 2005, lord chancellors also acted as the head of the judiciary and as the Speaker of the Lords. Today, those posts are held by others and the lord chancellor (Dominic Raab in 2022) is just a member of the cabinet and in charge of the Department of Justice.

Evidence of a lack of diversity among judges

REVISED

+ Under-representation of women: 17% (2 out of 12) in the UKSC in mid-2021, and 25% in the Court of Appeal in 2021.
+ Lack of black, Asian and minority ethnic (BAME) judges: none in the UKSC in mid-2021, and 8% of all judges in 2021 (up from 6% in 2014).
+ Fewer non-barristers, i.e. judges with a background as solicitors or legal executives: 32% of all judges in 2020, down from 37% in 2014.
+ Domination of public school and Oxbridge background, especially among the top levels of the judiciary: 11 of the 12 UKSC justices serving in mid-2021 studied at either Oxford or Cambridge.

Table 4.2 assesses whether a lack of diversity among the judiciary matters.

Table 4.2 Does a lack of diversity in the judiciary matter?

Yes	No
Judges do not reflect modern British society.	Unlike MPs, judges are not representatives of the people but are chosen for their professional expertise and on merit alone.
It could make it hard for judges to understand the cultural context of some cases fully.	Judges are not there to empathise but to apply the law neutrally and professionally.
There has been little improvement in judicial diversity in the last decade, especially at the top levels of the judicial bench.	Diversity is greater and growing lower down the judicial hierarchy. Changes at the top can only come about as the talent pool broadens lower down. It will alter eventually.
It reduces the public's trust in the judiciary and leads to biased 'pro-establishment' decisions.	The public would rather have judicial decisions in the hands of the best qualified. There is no evidence of an establishment bias. On the contrary, judges have often criticised governments and upheld the rights of minorities such as asylum seekers.
More input from democratically elected representatives in the appointments process would help bolster diversity.	This would almost inevitably lead to a dangerous politicisation of the judiciary.

> **Now test yourself** TESTED
>
> 1. Are judicial independence and judicial neutrality the same thing?
> 2. In what ways can the judiciary be said to lack diversity?
> 3. Explain what is meant by *ultra vires*.
>
> **Answers on p. 124**

> **Exam tip**
>
> Remember that the judges for the Supreme Court are *not* appointed by the JAC but by a slightly different procedure (see p. 47).

The UK Supreme Court

Key points

REVISED

- Set up in 2009 following the Constitutional Reform Act 2005.
- Replaced the Law Lords as the highest court in the land.
- Physically and institutionally separate from parliament, therefore embodying the notion of the separation of powers.
- Comprises 12 judges.
- To be eligible for appointment, candidates must have served for either a minimum of 2 years in a senior judicial role or 15 years as a barrister or solicitor.
- Its composition has been criticised for its lack of racial and gender diversity (see p. 45), although its president from 2017 to 2020 was Lady Hale.
- Judges enjoy permanent job security until reaching compulsory retirement age (70 in most cases). They cannot be removed by ministers or parliament unless for gross misconduct.
- Free of political pressure.

Main roles

REVISED

- The final court of appeal for all UK civil cases and criminal cases from England, Wales and Northern Ireland.
- Hears appeals on points of law from the general public and of national importance.
- Enforces the ECHR in the UK, which means it reduces the number of cases on behalf of UK citizens heard in the European Court of Human Rights (ECtHR) in Strasbourg.
- Acts as the final court of appeal for a number of British Overseas Territories and former colonies such as Jamaica.

> **Revision activity**
>
> Make notes on five key cases heard by the UKSC (either from those given in Table 4.3 below or researched from elsewhere) and write down whether or not (and why) a lack of diversity might have been relevant to each case.

> **Exam tip**
>
> Do not confuse the titles of the judges in the UKSC with peers in the House of Lords. Although all the UKSC judges are styled 'lord' or 'lady', these are courtesy titles only (which carry no wider rights such as membership of the House of Lords) and they are not life peers. In this respect, they are unlike the old Law Lords who were made life peers and could sit in the Lords and vote.

UKSC and Europe

REVISED

- Under the Human Rights Act 1998, the UKSC has the power to decide whether an action by a public body or particular law is in breach of the ECHR and issue a 'declaration of incompatibility'.
- Such declarations are relatively rare, but one was issued in 2018 finding that the government discriminated against different-sex couples by banning them from entering into civil partnerships as same-sex couples could. The government was found to have breached their rights under Article 14 (non-discrimination) and Article 8 (respect for private life). The law was subsequently changed.

- Although obliged to respect the precedents of the ECtHR, on rare occasions the UKSC has effectively sent cases back to Strasbourg for reconsideration, e.g. the 2009 Horncastle case. This case concerned the use of statements from witnesses not present in court and therefore unable to be cross-examined. While such evidence had been long accepted in British courts, the ECtHR ruled that a person convicted by such hearsay evidence had been denied access to a fair trial. The UKSC in effect disagreed with the ECtHR.
- The Horncastle case influenced the ECtHR when it came to hear a similar case two years later. Therefore, the UKSC is both influenced by and influences the ECtHR.
- Separate to the ECHR, the UKSC until Brexit had to take EU law into consideration when hearing cases that concerned European treaties to which the UK had signed up.
- Brexit affected only the UKSC and EU law, *not* the UKSC and the ECHR as the UK remains a signatory to the ECHR.

> **Exam tip**
>
> Be careful not to draw too many parallels between the UK Supreme Court and its namesake in the USA. The US Supreme Court has more powers because it interprets the codified and sovereign US constitution. In contrast, the UKSC must respect parliamentary sovereignty. It cannot 'strike down' Acts of Parliament as unconstitutional.

Appointment procedure

REVISED

- Designed to be non-political, independent and based on merit alone.
- Vacancies are filled by a special selection commission.
- The selection commission is made up of the president and deputy president of the court, and a member each from the Judicial Appointments Commission (which acts for England and Wales), the Judicial Appointments Board for Scotland and the Northern Ireland Judicial Appointments Commission. This reflects the fact that the court oversees the courts in all parts of the UK.
- The commission consults with certain senior judges (who do not wish to be appointed themselves) before putting forward a name selected on merit alone.
- The lord chancellor can accept or reject the nomination. They cannot put forward their own candidate.

Key cases

REVISED

Table 4.3 outlines some key cases that have been heard by the UKSC.

Table 4.3 A selection of key cases heard by the UKSC

Case	Key features	Outcome and significance
R (on the application of Miller and Dos Santos) v Secretary of State for Exiting the European Union [2017] The **Article 50** 'Brexit' Appeal	- Must the government get parliamentary approval to invoke Article 50 to leave the EU following the EU referendum? - Must the devolved assemblies be consulted about Article 50? - A case about important constitutional matters.	- Parliament must be allowed a vote on Article 50. - Devolved assemblies need not be consulted on Article 50. - The case reinforced the principle of parliamentary sovereignty and the supremacy of Westminster over devolved assemblies in such matters. - In part a victory and in part a defeat for the government. - Not a pro-Remain decision by the court, rather about interpreting the British constitution.
Great Ormond Street Hospital v *Yates and Gard* [2017] The Charlie Gard case	- Were the parents of a seriously ill baby (Charlie Gard) allowed to take him abroad for medical treatment? - The removal was opposed by both Great Ormond Street Hospital and Charlie's independent guardian on the legal grounds that it was not in his best interests. - A case involving medical ethics to some extent, but actually more about the legality of the procedures followed.	- The court found against Charlie's parents, who were not allowed to take him to the USA. - He died shortly afterwards when his life support was removed. - The case reaffirmed the principle that parents do not have the ultimate say on their child's care. - Although involving a matter of life and death, the case was not about morality or ethics but interpretation of the law and legal procedures.

Case	Key features	Outcome and significance
Commissioner of Police of the Metropolis v *DSD and another* [2018] The John Worboys ('Black Cab Rapist') case	+ Two victims of the serial rapist John Worboys successfully won a case against the Metropolitan Police for not taking their allegations seriously enough at the time. + They won substantial compensation. + A human rights case.	+ The UKSC decided that the victims' human rights had been breached. + If a police force conducts an investigation into a major crime that fails in a sufficiently serious way, it could be liable to a human rights action brought by the victim.
R (Miller) v *The Prime Minister* and *Cherry* v *Advocate General for Scotland* [2019] The prorogation of parliament case	+ In August 2019 new Prime Minister Boris Johnson sought to suspend (prorogue) parliament for a record length of time, five weeks. + This was achieved through royal prerogative and not a vote by parliament itself. Many MPs felt this gave parliament too little time to scrutinise Brexit legislation before the planned leaving date of 31 October. + The case was brought by Gina Miller, who had brought an earlier Brexit case in 2017. + A case involving the extent of prime ministerial power and the ability of parliament to debate and decide upon key issues. Also, it brought into the spotlight the function of the royal prerogative.	+ A defeat for the government. + The Supreme Court ruled unanimously that prorogation in these circumstances was unlawful. + The Supreme Court overruled the Appeal Court. It decided that courts did have the power to rule upon the use of the royal prerogative. + The UKSC ruled that the motives of the prime minister and the effects of prorogation frustrated and prevented the power of parliament to carry out its functions as a legislature and supervision of the executive. + The case represented a victory for the principle of constitutional sovereignty. + The ruling had little impact on the Brexit process, as Johnson subsequently called an election and won with a large majority.
Begum v *Special Immigration Appeals Commission and the Secretary of State for the Home Department* [2020] The Shamima Begum case	+ Shamima Begum had left the UK in 2015 to join the terrorist group ISIL in Syria. + She was subsequently stripped of her British citizenship but wanted to return to the UK to appeal the decision. This was upheld by the Court of Appeal, but overruled by the Supreme Court in February 2021 by a unanimous ruling. + A case concerning both human rights (to a fair trial/appeal) and the ability of higher courts to overrule lower courts.	+ A victory for the UK government; according to Home Secretary Priti Patel speaking on the BBC, the verdict: 'reaffirmed the home secretary's authority to make vital national security decisions'. + The higher court ruled against the findings of the lower court, the Appeal Court, arguing that they had erred on some legal aspects of the case. + The verdict was welcomed by those who emphasised national security (Begum had not fully recanted her support for ISIL) but was criticised by some human rights activists, not least given her age, 15, when she joined ISIL.

> **Making links**
>
> The prorogation case links in well with the topics of prime ministerial power, the functions of parliament and the UK constitution. It reaffirmed the principle of parliamentary sovereignty, clipped the powers of the prime minister and upheld the rights of parliament. It also gave rise to discussion on whether or not royal prerogative needed to be clarified and put on a clear legal basis.

> **Article 50** The process by which a member state can leave the EU.

> **Now test yourself** — TESTED
>
> 4 When was the UKSC set up?
> 5 Are UKSC judges appointed in the same way as other judges?
> 6 Explain the difference between EU law and the ECHR.
> 7 Where is the ECtHR located?
> 8 Must the British government accept all the decisions of the ECtHR?
> 9 What is the link between the UKSC and the ECHR?
> 10 On the whole, does the UKSC tend to support or oppose the UK government in its judgments?
>
> **Answers on p. 125**

> **Revision activity**
>
> Create a diagram that shows the respective powers of the UKSC, the ECtHR and the European Court of Justice, and where they overlap and where they are separate.

Impact on government, legislature and the making of policy

REVISED

- The UKSC acts as a significant check and balance on government and parliament in regard to both legislation and executive actions.
- Under the Human Rights Act 1998, all government bills must include a statement saying that, in the minister's view, the bill is either compatible with human rights or that it is incompatible but that the government nevertheless wishes to proceed with the bill. The UKSC may, of course, disagree in a subsequent court case that the bill was compatible. This makes governments more careful and cautious when drawing up bills.
- Sometimes, as with the 2019 prorogation of parliament, the judiciary appears to enter the political arena. In that case, however, it was upholding the notion of parliamentary sovereignty rather than asserting its own authority.
- On rare occasions, the UK government can choose to ignore the rulings of the ECtHR. In 2005, the court ruled that a blanket ban on denying all prisoners the vote was incompatible with the ECHR, but parliament did not subsequently change the law.
- Sometimes the UKSC comes close to overturning key aspects of government policy. For example, in 2015 the court only narrowly (by a 3-to-2 margin) upheld the controversial cap on the total amount of benefits an out-of-work family can receive, including housing benefit and benefits for children, to £500 per week. Opponents claimed it breached aspects of both the ECHR and the UN Convention on the Rights of the Child. Had the opponents won, it would have created a major headache for the government and seriously threatened both parliamentary sovereignty and democratic accountability.

Exam tip

Make sure you learn a small number of key cases where the UKSC has made important decisions. Ensure you know what category each falls under (e.g. human rights, the power of government, etc.). Use the internet and media to keep your examples up to date.

Summary

You should now have an understanding of:
- the meaning of the following key terms: judicial independence, judicial impartiality/neutrality, the separation of powers, *ultra vires* and judicial review
- how judges, including those of the UK Supreme Court, are appointed, and issues concerning the composition of the judiciary
- some of the key cases heard by the UK Supreme Court
- how the UK Supreme Court impacts on both government and parliament.

Exam skills

When answering questions about the UK judiciary, it is important to show knowledge of a range of landmark cases. Go beyond listing them — explain what they reveal about the power and role of the judiciary, especially the UKSC. Be careful not to exaggerate the extent to which it limits government. On many occasions, it upholds government actions.

Exam practice

1 Explain and analyse three key aspects of the UK judiciary. [9]
2 'The UKSC has become increasingly prominent and powerful in the political life of the nation.' Analyse and evaluate this statement. [25]

Answers available online

5 Devolution

Key points

+ Since 1999, the way the UK is run has been transformed by devolution.
+ Devolution is the delegation of power from the UK Parliament in Westminster to assemblies in Cardiff (Wales) and Belfast (Northern Ireland) and the Scottish Parliament in Edinburgh.
+ The Westminster Parliament is technically still able to pass laws for any part of the UK, but in practice only deals with devolved matters with the agreement of the devolved governments.

Devolved bodies in the UK

Roles, powers and responsibilities of devolved bodies

REVISED

The extent of the powers of devolved bodies varies somewhat from region to region, as shown in Table 5.1.

Table 5.1 Current UK devolved bodies and their powers

Devolved body	Location	Number of members	Voting system	Key powers (selected examples)	Examples of areas where it lacks powers	Leader of the government (mid-2021)
Scottish Parliament	Edinburgh (Holyrood)	129	Additional Member System (AMS)	Agriculture Environment Income tax Education Health Transport Justice, policing and courts	Foreign policy Brexit negotiations Defence and national security Trade and industry	Nicola Sturgeon (SNP)
Senedd Cymru (Welsh Parliament)	Cardiff	60	AMS	Agriculture Environment Education Health Transport Fire and rescue services	Foreign policy Brexit negotiations Defence and national security	Mark Drakeford (Labour)
Northern Ireland Assembly*	Belfast (Stormont)	90	Single Transferable Vote (STV)	Agriculture Environment Education Health Transport Enterprise, trade and investment	Income tax Foreign policy Brexit negotiations Defence and national security	Vacant as of February 2022

Check your understanding and progress at www.hoddereducation.co.uk/myrevisionnotesdownloads

*As part of the Good Friday Agreement, uniquely in Ulster executive power must be shared between the two largest parties, i.e. in reality a unionist and a nationalist party. This is to avoid power being held solely by the majority community. The clause is designed to avoid sectarian discrimination and ensure power is shared between the two communities.

> **Exam tip**
>
> Devolution is not the same as federalism, where power is permanently transferred to regional assemblies or states, as in the USA. In theory, Westminster could take back the powers of the devolved assemblies.

Key dates

REVISED

1997 Tony Blair's Labour government holds referendums in Scotland and Wales over devolution. Both vote in favour, albeit by a very small margin in Wales.

1998 The Good Friday Agreement leads to a ceasefire and an end to the Troubles in Northern Ireland, paving the way for a Northern Ireland Assembly.

1999 Devolved assemblies are set up in Wales and Scotland.

2011 A referendum in Wales supports the transfer of greater powers by a large margin (63% to 37%).

2012 The Scotland Act devolves some tax-raising powers (e.g. income tax) to the Scottish Parliament and allows it to borrow up to £2 billion a year.

2014 Scotland rejects full independence in a referendum (55% to 45%). The Wales Act grants more powers to the Welsh government including stamp duty, business rates and landfill tax.

2016 The Scotland Act devolves further powers including control over road signs and onshore oil extraction, and to change its electoral system, with a two-thirds vote by the Scottish Parliament.

2017 The Northern Ireland Assembly is suspended due to a breakdown in relations between the two largest parties, the DUP (unionist) and Sinn Féin (nationalist). Suspension only ended in January 2020.

The Wales Act gives further powers to Cardiff, largely similar to those granted to Scotland in 2016 but excluding the power to set income tax rates/bands.

2019 Welsh government allowed to vary income tax rates.

2020 Welsh Assembly uses its powers under the 2017 Wales Act to change its name to Senedd Cymru or Welsh Parliament.

The Troubles The period from the late 1960s when much of Northern Ireland was affected by terrorism including bombings and assassinations carried out by terrorists from both communities: Unionist/Protestant who wanted Ulster to remain part of the UK and Catholic/Nationalist who wanted a united Ireland. These terrorists belonged to groups such as the Provisional IRA or the Ulster Defence Association (UDA).

Stamp duty A tax payable when buying property.

> **Exam tip**
>
> Given the extent of powers now in the hands of the devolved assemblies, the UK system of government can be referred to as quasi federal rather than unitary.

Table 5.2 examines some of the arguments about how well devolution worked in the regions.

Table 5.2 Has devolution worked in the regions?

Yes	No
It has strengthened the union; Scotland voted to remain in the UK in the 2014 referendum. It has given them the 'best of both worlds'.	The results of the 2014 referendum were close, and many in Scotland want a second vote. Devolution has shown that the regions can run many of their own affairs well without Westminster.
The powers of the devolved assemblies have been expanded since 1999.	This has been far more limited in Northern Ireland.
It has consolidated the peace process in Northern Ireland.	Tensions in Northern Ireland remain. In 2021, for example, there were violent protests against the Northern Ireland Protocol, part of the Brexit agreement.
It has enabled greater legislative autonomy for the regions and enabled them to adopt policies best suited to the area.	It has created unevenness across the UK, for example with student tuition fees and NHS prescriptions. Covid-19 regulations also varied across the nation during the pandemic.

Devolution in England

England is the only region of the UK not to have devolved assemblies. This means that devolution in the UK is termed asymmetrical. Instead, it has various tiers of local government with different degrees of power and responsibility.

Asymmetrical Uneven and not the same across the whole nation.

Local government

REVISED

- Single-tier unitary authorities carry out all functions of local government. These are mostly in large cities and urban areas such as Birmingham and Portsmouth.
- Two-tier local councils comprise county councils and district councils. Here, functions are split between the two types of local authority. They are found mainly in more rural and less densely populated areas.
- Among the key functions of English local government are the provision of education, social care, waste collection and social housing.
- Nine large cities or regions (Greater Manchester, Liverpool City Region, West Midlands, West of England, Tees Valley, Cambridgeshire and Peterborough, Sheffield City Region, North of Tyne, and West Yorkshire) now have directly elected 'metro mayors' such as Andy Burnham (Greater Manchester) who serve several combined local authorities. The government's Devolution Deals allow combined authorities to take on additional responsibilities, but require a metro mayor to be elected for that area.

Unitary authorities Where a single council carries out all the functions of local authorities, including major ones such as education and social care undertaken elsewhere by county councils.

Exam tip

Do not confuse the nine metro mayors with traditional mayors that councils have already. Metro mayors are combined authority mayors who are voted for by the electorate in the area. Traditional mayors hold office for one year only and the post is ceremonial with no decision-making powers.

Making links

Devolution is a good example of a major constitutional change made since 1997, and links in with the UK constitution topic covered in Chapter 1.

Limits on local government

REVISED

Unlike the devolved assemblies, local councils are severely limited in what they can do on their own initiative:

- They have very limited legislative powers although they can, in some circumstances, introduce certain measures such as congestion charges in London.
- Most functions that involve carrying out responsibilities and roles are decided by central government.
- Most revenue-raising is tightly controlled by central government. For example, council tax cannot be raised beyond a limit set by Westminster (5% in 2021) without a local referendum being held. Only one such referendum has ever been held and the council tax rise was rejected by voters.

Debate around devolution for England

REVISED

With the rise of devolved assemblies elsewhere in the UK, there has been some discussion around whether there should be an English Parliament or regional assemblies, as shown in Table 5.3.

Table 5.3 Arguments for and against an English Parliament or regional assemblies

Arguments for	Arguments against
+ It would be a logical extension of the creation of devolved assemblies, which on the whole have worked well and proved popular.	+ England lacks the national identity of Scotland, Wales or Northern Ireland.
+ It would bring parity across the UK regarding devolution.	+ There is no widespread support for such a measure. A referendum in 2004 to set up an elected assembly for the northeast was decisively rejected 78% to 22%.
+ Regional assemblies would enable decision making to be brought closer to voters and reduce the dominance of London.	+ England is much larger in terms of population than any of the other regions. No other country with a federal or semi-federal system has one region that is so dominant within the whole nation.
+ An English Parliament would resolve the West Lothian question, whereby Scottish, Welsh and Northern Irish MPs currently have a vote on matters that affect only England, whereas MPs from England are unable to vote on matters that have been devolved.	+ Regional assemblies would add extra cost and bureaucracy to the UK political system.
+ An English Parliament could be located away from the capital (e.g. in Birmingham) and thus reduce London's current dominance of politics and the media.	+ There are other ways to resolve the West Lothian question, such as English votes for English laws (EVEL). Under EVEL an extra stage was introduced in the middle of the law-making process, allowing English MPs to block anything they did not like in bills deemed to be 'England only'. EVEL was abolished in July 2021, however, as the government argued it was complex and time-consuming to the legislative process.
+ It would allow an alternative electoral system to be used, as is the case elsewhere in the UK, and therefore resolve the issue of electoral reform.	+ An English Parliament would raise the issue of what the role and purpose of the Westminster Parliament is, which could lead to more conflict between the UK and English prime ministers.
	+ Electoral reform is a separate issue and English devolution should not be created just to achieve it.

Making links

The ease with which EVEL was ended is a good example of the flexibility of the British constitution due to parliamentary sovereignty, covered in Chapter 1. This contrasts with the formal rigidity of the American constitution, which is covered in the companion MRN book *US and Comparative Politics*.

Now test yourself

TESTED

1 Look at the following statements about devolution in the UK and decide whether each is true or false.
   a The devolved assemblies all have equal powers.
   b Devolution in Northern Ireland is slightly different to that in Scotland and Wales.
   c Devolution has seen more powers transferred away from Westminster over the last 20 or so years.
   d English local government represents a form of devolution.
   e Devolved assemblies use different electoral systems to those used for UK general elections.
2 What is the West Lothian question?
3 Which sort of places are likely to have unitary authorities?
4 What does EVEL stand for, and was it successful?
5 Name a region that has a directly elected metro mayor.
6 What were held before devolution was introduced?

Answers on p. 125

The impact of devolution on the UK government

Key points

- Devolution has reduced the power of Westminster as many areas of government are now the responsibility of devolved assemblies.
- It raises the issue of English devolution and the West Lothian question.
- It has led the government to transfer more powers to some English local authorities via combined authorities and metro mayors.
- It has not weakened (in theory at least) the concept of Westminster sovereignty. Devolved assemblies have their powers delegated, not inalienably transferred. In reality, however, it is highly unlikely that devolution would ever be reversed.
- It has created more variation across the UK. For example, prescriptions are free in Wales and Scotland, and those earning over £150,000 pay 1% more income tax in Scotland.

> **Exam tip**
>
> Ensure you distinguish between proposals for a single English Parliament and for a number of English regional assemblies. Both come under the heading of English devolution but they are different approaches.

> **Revision activity**
>
> Using the arguments for and against further devolution for England, together with any other relevant points from your own notes, create two word maps that show the relative importance of points on each side of the argument.

> **Summary**
>
> You should now have an understanding of:
> - the current structure and powers of local government/devolution in England
> - how devolution has developed and expanded since 1997
> - the main powers of the devolved assemblies in Scotland, Wales and Northern Ireland
> - the arguments for and against further devolution in England and setting up an English Parliament
> - how the devolved assemblies have affected the Westminster Parliament.

> **Exam skills**
>
> Most essay questions about this topic will probably ask you to evaluate how successful devolution has been. It is important here to consider the complex aspects of success. For example, to a nationalist, devolution can be reckoned a success if it furthers the cause of independence. To a supporter of keeping the UK intact, devolution would be viewed as a success if it makes the union stronger.
>
> The evidence is quite finely balanced, especially in Scotland where the 2014 referendum result could be interpreted in two ways: as a victory for unionists, or as showing how much support for Scottish independence there is. The SNP's recent dominance of Scottish politics also needs to be analysed carefully. Not everyone who votes SNP will necessarily be a passionate advocate for Scottish independence, though many are.
>
> In any essay, it is important to consider the evidence in a cautious way, avoiding statements that are too definitive, such as: 'The outcome of the 2014 referendum on Scottish independence shows that devolution has been a success, as the Scots rejected full independence.' Aim for a more nuanced approach, such as: 'The outcome of the 2014 referendum on Scottish independence shows that devolution could be viewed as both a success and a failure depending on one's perspective and interpretation of the result.' You would then need to develop that point in more detail.

Exam practice

1 'Devolution in the UK has been a resounding success.' Analyse and evaluate this statement. [25]

> Twenty years ago on Monday, the newly devolved Scottish parliament met in Edinburgh for the first time. It heard a speech from the late Donald Dewar that can still send tingles down the spine. The opening, said Scotland's new first minister, was 'the day when democracy was renewed in Scotland, when we revitalised our place in this our United Kingdom'.
>
> At the weekend, the Queen led ceremonies at the Holyrood building to mark the anniversary. There is no question that the Scottish parliament is now, 'at the centre of public life'. But the belief of the founders in 1999 that the devolved parliament would revitalise the union seems far more questionable. Twenty years on, the issue is more fraught, and the union is more fragile.
>
> Along with the new Welsh Assembly, which was established at the same time but with fewer powers, the setting up of the Scottish parliament was the most significant step in constitutional devolution within the United Kingdom since the setting up of Stormont in 1921. Devolution to Scotland took place in response to political pressures that faced the UK government of the day.
>
> In all these cases, devolution was an asymmetrical process. A constitutional change was made to the affected part of the UK that did not directly impinge on the rest. Each act of devolution was an attempt to answer a particular perceived need in that part of the UK without at the same time challenging the sovereignty of the Westminster Parliament or raising questions about the government and parliamentary representation of England.
>
> Part of the union's problem today is that Mr Dewar and others miscalculated. They thought devolution would persuade the Scots to turn their backs on independence. They thought a parliament elected by proportional representation would ensure the SNP could never win a majority. In the event, the SNP won one in 2011, came close to winning the vote for independence in 2014 and still commands the field. Against the backdrop of a Brexit that most Scots opposed, the nationalist cause has prospered.
>
> But in truth the biggest threat to the union lies in England. The UK's largest nation, and 85% of the UK's inhabitants, have little systemic devolution of any kind. While other UK nations enjoy forms of self-government and civil societies of notable vibrancy, England as such does not. The English have no effective self-government at local, regional or national level. Instead, they have a UK parliament elected by first-past-the-post, which stifles minority parties and whose large parties have a built-in interest to resist change. The union is in danger, but the danger is not primarily from Scotland, Wales or Northern Ireland. It mostly comes from England itself.
>
> Source: The *Guardian*, 30 June 2019

2 Read the above extract. Analyse, evaluate and compare the arguments in the extract for and against the view that devolution has worked poorly in the UK. [25]

Answers available online

6 Democracy and participation

Key points

REVISED

+ The UK is a representative democracy.
+ Before 1918, all women and many men could not vote. Groups such as the Chartists, the Suffragists and the Suffragettes campaigned for change. Today, there are demands for voting rights for prisoners and for 16- and 17-year-olds.
+ In a healthy democracy, people vote in elections, join political parties and engage politically with important issues. Some fear that modern Britain is experiencing a participation crisis as fewer people are getting involved in politics.

> **Democracy** A system of government in which the people have ultimate power. The term 'democracy' means 'rule by the people'.

Democracy

Nature of democracy

REVISED

The word democracy comes from the Greek words *demos* ('the people') and *kratia* ('rule by'). The concept of 'rule by the people' originated in Greece around the fifth century BC. Athenians used direct democracy but modern Western democracies use representative democracy.

> **Direct democracy** A system of democracy in which the people make decisions, not the government. Votes take place on specific questions.
>
> **Representative democracy** A system of democracy in which people vote for elected representatives. These elected representatives make decisions on the people's behalf.

Table 6.1 outlines the features of democracy.

Table 6.1 The features of democracy

Feature	Description
Representation	People's opinions are represented to the government.
Participation	People participate in politics. This can be through voting, joining political parties or pressure groups, or lobbying their elected representatives or the government.
Accountability	The government is accountable to the people. If the electorate thinks the government has done a bad job, it can vote in a different government.
Legitimacy	The government has legitimacy (legal authority) because it has been chosen by the people.
Rule of law	The country's laws apply equally to everyone and anyone who breaks the law is punished.
Elections	People vote regularly in elections. These may be to elect representatives (representative democracy) or to directly decide on specific issues (direct democracy).
Smooth transition of power	There is a formal process for handing power from one government to the next and this takes place peacefully.
Civil rights	People have their rights protected by law.
Education and information	The public are politically educated and have access to accurate information from trustworthy sources.

Check your understanding and progress at www.hoddereducation.co.uk/myrevisionnotesdownloads

Different types of democracy

REVISED

Direct democracy

- Direct democracy means that people vote 'yes' or 'no' on specific questions.
- This is different from representative democracy, in which people vote for representatives to make decisions on their behalf.
- No modern country makes every decision using direct democracy. This would be too difficult with big populations.
- Switzerland has the most directly democratic system. Its citizens vote frequently on a wide range of questions and they can propose initiatives to change the law. The USA also uses ballot initiatives and referendums at state level.
- Elements of direct democracy are used increasingly in the UK, including referendums and petitions.

Table 6.2 compares the advantages and disadvantages of direct democracy.

Table 6.2 Advantages and disadvantages of direct democracy

Advantages	Disadvantages
+ People can participate directly in the decision-making process. + The wishes of the people cannot be ignored by their elected representatives or the government. + People can be motivated to become well-informed about political issues. + Decisions have the direct authority of the people. This gives them greater legitimacy.	+ The public may not fully understand the question they are voting on. Elected representatives might be better placed to analyse and evaluate the issue. + The majority of people may vote for something that undermines the rights of a minority group. This is known as the tyranny of the majority. + People may vote for emotional or populist short-term reasons, rather than taking a more considered view. + Holding so many votes is slow and expensive, particularly in countries with large populations.

Representative government

- Almost all modern Western democracies use representative government.
- Regular elections are held so that people can elect representatives.
- In the UK there are separate national and local elections.
- These elected representatives become part of a legislative assembly that makes laws.
- A government is also elected, either directly (as in a presidential democracy such as the USA) or indirectly (as in a parliamentary democracy such as the UK).
- Some elected representatives follow the delegate model (see p. 25), in which they vote according to how they think their constituents would wish them to.
- Others follow the trustee model (see p. 24) developed by Edmund Burke (1729–97), who argued that MPs should vote according to their best judgement, as they have a better understanding of the issues than their constituents.
- Most Western representative democracies are liberal democracies.

Presidential democracy A democracy in which the executive (government) is directly elected by the people.

Parliamentary democracy A democracy in which the executive is not directly elected by the people. Instead, the executive is formed by whichever party has the greatest support in the legislature (parliament).

Liberal democracies Types of representative democracy in which the rule of law is followed, the freedom of citizens is protected by the government and many different political parties compete freely to win power.

Revision activity

Using the information given in Table 7.6 (p. 77) on the 2016 EU referendum, add examples for each of the advantages and disadvantages listed in Table 6.2.

> **Exam tip**
>
> Do not assume that the UK's use of referendums makes it a direct democracy rather than a representative democracy. It remains a representative democracy in which MPs are elected to make decisions on the people's behalf. The increasing use of referendums since 1997 (see Table 7.6 on p. 77) means that the UK has become a more participatory democracy (one in which the public participate actively in decision making).

> **Making links**
>
> The UK constitution reflects the importance of representative democracy. Parliament is sovereign, and, since the 1911 Parliament Act, the House of Commons has been able to overrule the House of Lords. This means that the people's elected representatives — the MPs — hold sovereign power.

> **Exam tip**
>
> Make sure you fully understand the different types of democracy and how they apply to the UK. You can make synoptic links from all the other topics on the specification to democracy (e.g. pressure groups and pluralism, parliament and representative democracy, the EU and direct democracy), so be prepared to use democracy as a synoptic link in other questions on the UK exam paper.

> **Now test yourself** TESTED
>
> 1 What does 'democracy' mean?
> 2 Name as many features of democracy as you can.
> 3 What is the difference between direct democracy and representative democracy?
> 4 Give two examples of modern Western democracies that use elements of direct democracy.
> 5 What are the advantages and disadvantages of representative democracy?
>
> **Answers on p. 125**

How suffrage has changed since the Great Reform Act 1832

REVISED

Suffrage is the right to vote, also referred to as the franchise. Table 6.3 summarises how suffrage has changed in the UK.

Table 6.3 How has suffrage changed in the UK?

Key date and Act	Significance
Before 1832	Only rich, male landowners could vote
	Fewer than 4% of the population
Great Reform Act 1832	One in five male adults could vote
	5.6% of the total population
Second Reform Act 1867	Much bigger in scope than the Great Reform Act
	Allowed working-class men in cities to vote if they met a property qualification
	Doubled the size of the electorate
Third Reform Act 1884	All working men who met a property qualification could vote
	40% of adult men still excluded
Representation of the People Act 1918	A product of the social and political changes caused by the First World War
	All men over the age of 21 (or 19 for veterans) could vote
	Women over 30 who met the property qualification could vote
Representation of the People Act 1928	Women finally received the vote on equal terms to men
	All men and women over 21 could vote
	Property qualifications removed
Representation of the People Act 1969	Voting age lowered to 18

> **Exam tip**
>
> Do not claim that women won the vote in 1918; the reality was rather more complicated. *Some* women (those over 30 who met the property qualification) won the vote in 1918, but the rest had to wait until 1928 to receive the franchise on the same terms as men.

Debates regarding universal suffrage

REVISED

Gender

- Women were traditionally seen as the 'weaker sex', both physically and mentally.
- They were not considered to have sufficient education or intelligence to be trusted with the vote.
- Opponents of women's suffrage in the nineteenth and early twentieth centuries argued that women were too emotional to vote rationally.
- Traditionalists felt that a woman's place was in the home, tending to her family. Politics would distract her.

Class

- The wealthy elite who held the franchise before 1832 worried that their power would be reduced if people from other classes had the vote.
- There were fears that working-class men were too poorly educated to understand political issues.
- Some feared the working class would support socialism, threatening the economic welfare of other classes.
- The contribution and sacrifice of working-class men during the First World War meant that denying them the vote could no longer be justified.

Ethnicity

- There were (and are) no ethnic qualifications for voting in the UK.
- People of colour have historically been underrepresented in Parliament.
- Black and Asian voters were less likely than the general population to register to vote in 2019.

> **Making links**
>
> The Electoral Reform Society is a pressure group. It dates back to 1884 and describes itself as the longest-standing pro-democracy organisation in the world. It opposes the 'first-past-the-post' electoral system and campaigns for proportional representation using the Single Transferable Vote system.

Age

- Younger people were not seen as having sufficient political education, independence or maturity. People aged 18 to 20 years old only received the vote in 1969.
- Young women aged 21 to 29 were denied the vote in 1918, despite their contribution to the war effort. They were considered more emotional and unstable than older women.
- Today, there is a campaign to give 16- and 17-year-olds the vote.
- 16- and 17-year-olds were allowed to vote in the 2014 Scottish independence referendum, as it was recognised that the referendum result would affect the rest of their lives. They had a higher turnout than 18- to 24-year-olds.
- 16- and 17-year-olds can vote in elections for the Scottish Parliament and local councils, and for the Welsh Parliament (Senedd).
- The Labour Party, the Scottish National Party (SNP), the Liberal Democrats, Plaid Cymru and the Green Party all support the Votes at 16 campaign, as does the Electoral Reform Society.

> **Making links**
>
> The enfranchisement of Scottish and Welsh 16-year-olds is a good example of how devolution has caused variation in the rights of UK citizens. English and Northern Irish 16-year-olds cannot vote. Scottish prisoners serving less than 12 months can vote, but this is not the case in the rest of the UK.
>
> The Conservative Party's resistance to votes at 16 may be influenced by young people's voting behaviour. In the 2019 general election, voters under the age of 39 were more likely to vote Labour.

> **Exam tip**
>
> In a question on the development of suffrage, make sure you emphasise the importance of class as well as gender. Many working-class men were excluded from the franchise until 1918, just as women were.

> **Revision activity**
>
> 1 Make two lists: one giving arguments in favour of 16- and 17-year-olds having the vote, and one giving arguments against.
>
> 2 Should 16- and 17-year-olds be given the vote in all UK elections? Write a paragraph to summarise your opinion.

Significance of Chartists, Suffragists and Suffragettes

Table 6.4 outlines the significance of three groups: Chartists, Suffragists and Suffragettes.

Table 6.4 Chartists, Suffragists and Suffragettes

Group	Methods	Significance
Chartists (1838–48)	+ The Chartist movement was set up after the Great Reform Act 1832. + They campaigned for votes for all men over 21, secret ballots, no property qualifications for MPs, pay for MPs, equal-size constituencies and yearly elections to parliament. + The movement presented three petitions signed by millions to parliament.	+ All three petitions were rejected by parliament. + Authorities dealt harshly with unrest provoked by the rejection of the petitions. + The movement lacked a single leader and struggled to co-ordinate different groups across the nation. + Some Chartists called for violence, which caused many middle-class supporters to leave the movement, resulting in less money for campaigning. + The movement died out, but the Second and Third Reform Acts were passed in 1867 and 1884. + Today, all the Chartists' aims have been met apart from yearly elections.
Suffragists (1860s–1918)	+ Suffragists had campaigned for the vote since the 1860s. + In 1897 they formed the National Union of Women's Suffrage Societies (NUWSS). + Suffragists campaigned for the vote using peaceful constitutional methods (e.g. petitions, speeches, marches and letter-writing).	+ Despite decades of campaigning, women were no closer to getting the vote by 1903, which resulted in the formation of the Suffragettes. + The NUWSS had more than 100,000 members by 1914. + Leader Millicent Fawcett said their movement was 'like a glacier, slow-moving but unstoppable'.
Suffragettes (1903–14)	+ Frustrated with the Suffragists' lack of progress, Emmeline Pankhurst formed a rival organisation, the Women's Social and Political Union (WSPU), in 1903. + Suffragettes used militant methods including window breaking, chaining themselves to railings and arson. + Suffragettes received harsh prison sentences, which they attempted to reduce by hunger striking.	+ Suffragettes were dealt with harshly by the police and the government, including being force-fed in prison. + They attracted national attention and coverage in newspapers. + They were criticised by the Suffragists for using increasingly extreme methods.

Check your understanding and progress at www.hoddereducation.co.uk/myrevisionnotesdownloads

Group	Methods	Significance
	+ Emily Davison was killed in 1913 when she intercepted the king's horse at the Derby. + Leader Christabel Pankhurst went into hiding in France to avoid arrest. + The movement called off their campaign when war broke out in 1914.	+ The government refused to 'give in' to violence. + Many key supporters left the movement in protest over the arson campaign; membership numbers and funding fell. + Some argue that women won the vote in 1918 through their war service, not because of the Suffragettes. + It is likely that the government was eager to avoid a return to violence when they enfranchised women in 1918.

> **Exam tip**
>
> Do not confuse the Chartists with the Suffragists or Suffragettes. The Chartists were a mid-nineteenth century group that campaigned for male suffrage, whereas both the Suffragists and Suffragettes campaigned for female suffrage. The Suffragists date from the 1860s, whereas the Suffragettes — who were prepared to use much more militant methods — date from 1903.

Suffrage as a human right

REVISED

+ In 2005, the European Court of Human Rights ruled that denying all prisoners the right to vote violated their human rights.
+ The case in question, *Hirst v UK* [2005], involved a prisoner, John Hirst, who was serving a sentence for manslaughter. He argued that the UK government was in breach of the Human Rights Act 1998, which incorporated the European Convention on Human Rights into UK law. The case was initially dismissed by the UK High Court, but Hirst appealed to the European Court of Human Rights where he was successful. The UK government did not comply with the ruling.
+ Pressure groups such as the Howard League for Penal Reform and the Prison Reform Trust have campaigned for the government to obey the court's ruling.
+ Legally, the court has made it clear that voting is a human right.
+ However, many people believe that voting is a privilege that should be removed if someone commits a crime.
+ In 2017 the Conservative government announced plans to allow a small number of prisoners to vote (around 100) in order to compromise with the European Court of Human Rights.
+ In 2020 the Scottish Parliament passed legislation that gave prisoners serving 12 months or less the right to vote.

> **Now test yourself** TESTED
>
> 6 In which year did Britain first have universal suffrage?
> 7 Name the Chartists' six demands.
> 8 What was the main difference between the Suffragists and the Suffragettes?
> 9 Which political parties support the Votes at 16 campaign?
>
> **Answers on p. 125**

Participation

Is there a participation crisis?

REVISED

Participation is crucial to any democracy, but the UK may be experiencing a participation crisis. Some of the arguments for and against this are examined in Tables 6.5, 6.6 and 6.7. Figure 6.1 shows the turnout figures for recent UK general elections and the 2016 EU referendum.

> **Participation** People's involvement in political activity. It includes voting, writing to an MP, joining a political party or pressure group, standing for office, protesting and signing a petition.

Table 6.5 Turnout: arguments for and against a participation crisis

Arguments for	Arguments against
+ Turnout in general elections has fallen in recent decades. In 1950 more than 80% of the electorate voted. In 2001 just 59% did, a record low. + Some elections had even worse turnout — in the 2012 Police and Crime Commissioner (PCC) elections, just 15% of the electorate voted — the lowest turnout in a nationwide election in peacetime. This climbed to 27% in 2016 and 33% in 2021, but remains very low. The 2019 European Parliament elections had a turnout of just 37%. Turnout to the Welsh Parliament (Senedd) has never reached 50%, from the first elections in 1999 to those in 2021.	+ Turnout in general elections has been rising since 2001, reaching a high of 69% in the 2017 general election. The 67% turnout in the 2019 general election was the second highest since 1997. + Turnout in recent referendums has also been high. Some 85% voted in the 2014 Scottish independence referendum, and 72% in the 2016 EU referendum. + The contrast between the PCC elections and the EU and Scottish referendums shows that the electorate is selective: if people care about an issue, they will participate.

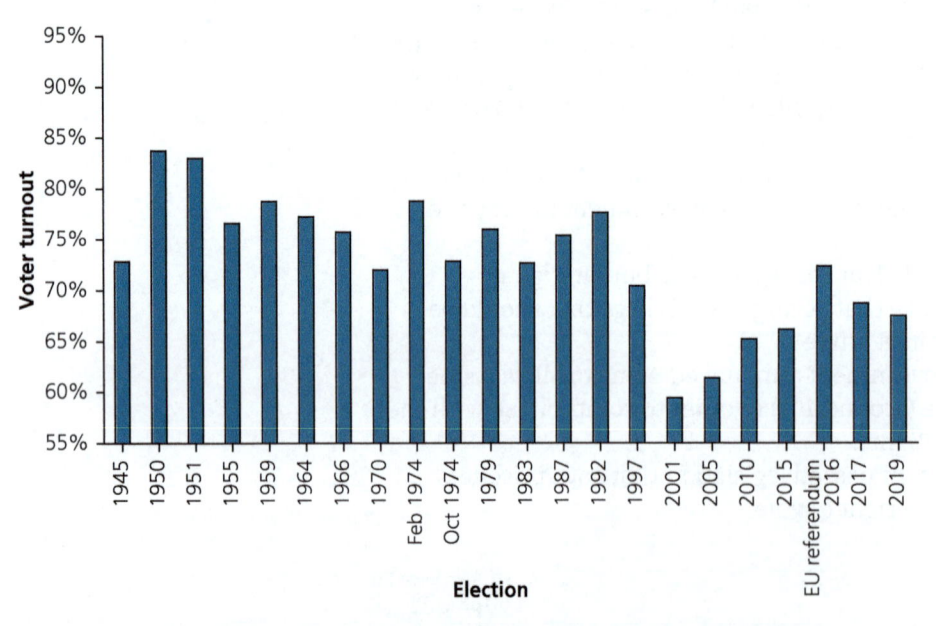

Figure 6.1 Turnout figures for UK general elections and the 2016 EU referendum

Table 6.6 Party membership: arguments for and against a participation crisis

Arguments for	Arguments against
+ Party membership has fallen since the 1950s, when the Conservatives had more than 2.5 million members and the Labour Party more than 1 million. In 2018 the Conservatives had just 124,000 members.	+ The membership of some parties has increased in recent years: Labour has over 500,000 members and the SNP membership more than quadrupled following the 2014 independence referendum, reaching over 125,000 in 2019. Conservative membership numbers had climbed back to 200,000 by 2021, and the Liberal Democrats had more than 115,000 members. + Minor parties have done very well over the last decade and more: UKIP won the 2014 European Parliament elections and received 3.9 million votes in the 2015 general election, the Brexit Party won the 2019 European Parliament elections, and the Green Party won its first seat in Parliament in 2010 and its highest ever number of Greens on local councils in 2021.

Check your understanding and progress at www.hoddereducation.co.uk/myrevisionnotesdownloads

Table 6.7 Changes in participation: arguments for and against a participation crisis

Arguments for	Arguments against
+ **Partisan dealignment** means that people increasingly feel no affiliation to any political party. + **Trade unions** have fewer members and are less powerful than in the 1980s. + Political apathy appears to be commonplace among young people. Turnout data for 18- to 24-year-olds shows they are less politically engaged than any other age group. + Disillusionment with politicians and political figures increased as a result of the 2009 expenses scandal, and has been maintained by scandals such as the 2020 Dominic Cummings affair in which a government adviser was caught breaking coronavirus restrictions, and the 2021–22 'Partygate' affair, in which Boris Johnson's government was investigated for a series of parties held during lockdowns. + 'Slacktivism' describes the tendency for people to participate in a superficial way by 'liking' or sharing political content online.	+ Pressure group membership has increased, so people are participating without needing to join a political party. + Social media and the internet has changed the nature of political participation. Pressure groups and political parties use social media to reach the public, co-ordinate their campaigns and raise money. + Internet-based movements can be powerful: more than 210,000 people joined the UK Black Lives Matter protests of summer 2020, with millions more participating online. This triggered a national debate about structural racism and how black history is taught in schools. Many schools subsequently rewrote their curriculum.

Partisan dealignment The process by which the electorate has become less strongly affiliated to political parties. It is reflected by falling party membership numbers and an increase in the number of floating voters.

Trade unions Organisations made up of workers, which campaign for better working conditions.

Pluralism Political philosophy that emphasises the benefits of many different groups influencing the decision-making process.

Making links

Participation is important for **pluralism**. In a pluralist democracy, many different groups and voices influence government. This should lead to more democratic decisions that represent the wishes of a broad range of society.

Exam tip

Do not confuse class dealignment and partisan dealignment. Class dealignment is a trend for voting to be less dependent on class. In the 1950s, middle-class voters tended to vote Conservative and working-class voters Labour, but they are now less closely aligned. Partisan dealignment is the process by which individuals are less likely to support a political party at all.

Increasing participation

REVISED

Suggested methods for increasing participation include:
+ votes at 16
+ online voting
+ compulsory voting
+ changing the electoral system so that everyone's vote counts equally
+ adopting a proportional electoral system, which would benefit minor parties and give voters more choice
+ increasing political education in schools
+ reducing the membership fees of political parties
+ more direct democracy.

Revision activity

Read the suggestions for increasing political participation and make a note of the advantages and disadvantages for each. Rank the suggestions in order of effectiveness (start with the one you think would be the most effective).

> **Exam tip**
>
> Examiners are looking for detailed examples, so be sure to learn the most recent turnout and membership figures. Your analysis will be much stronger if you support it with evidence.

> **Now test yourself** TESTED
>
> 10 How have methods of participation changed in recent years?
> 11 What is meant by partisan dealignment?
> 12 What is meant by 'slacktivism'?
> 13 Which political parties have seen significant membership growth in recent years?
> 14 What was the turnout for the 2014 Scottish Independence referendum, and for the 2016 EU referendum?
>
> **Answers on p. 125–6**

> **Exam skills**
>
> **Synoptic links**
>
> Essays that do not include synoptic points are limited to a Level 4 in the mark scheme and cannot reach the top (Level 5). Questions on democracy or participation provide plenty of opportunities to make synoptic links, including to:
> - electoral systems: some argue that proportional representation is more democratic than first-past-the-post (FPTP)
> - pressure groups: offer an alternative to conventional political participation and promote pluralism by representing the views of many different people to government
> - devolution: 16- and 17-year-olds can vote in Scotland and Wales, but not in the rest of the UK
> - political parties: the Conservatives remain a staunch supporter of FPTP, unlike most other parties
> - parliament: within our representative democracy, parliament is sovereign and MPs have a duty to represent their constituents effectively

> **Summary**
>
> You should now have an understanding of:
> - the nature of democracy, including its key features
> - the difference between direct and representative democracy
> - how the franchise has been extended from 1832 to the present
> - historical debates regarding who should have the vote and the modern debate over votes at 16
> - the significance of the Chartists, Suffragists and Suffragettes in campaigning for increased suffrage
> - the controversy over whether voting is a human right
> - how to justify whether you think prisoners should be allowed to vote
> - the extent to which the UK has a participation crisis
> - suggestions as to how participation levels could be increased.

Check your understanding and progress at www.hoddereducation.co.uk/myrevisionnotesdownloads

Exam practice

1. Explain and analyse three ways in which the Suffragettes were significant in the campaign to extend the franchise. [9]

2. Read the following extract.

> In recent years, there has been much discussion of the phenomenon of partisan dealignment. It was argued that the falling membership figures of the main political parties was evidence of a long-term trend of political disengagement by the electorate. There is some truth to this: the membership figures of the Conservatives, for example, stood at 200,000 in 2021, a far cry from their 2.5 million members in the 1950s. Class dealignment and the fall in trade union membership have meant that age, rather than class, has become the dominant factor that predicts how people vote. This was the case in the 2014 Scottish independence referendum, the 2016 EU referendum and the 2017 and 2019 general elections. Many people are floating voters who change party from election to election, and many potential voters do not bother to turnout. The days in which political parties could depend on legions of committed regular voters are over.
>
> However, this analysis is over-simplistic. Firstly, it ignores the evidence that some smaller parties have seen significant increases in membership. UKIP had fewer than 15,000 members in 2008, and this had more than doubled to 34,000 in 2017. The newly formed Brexit Party was able to win the European Parliament elections in 2019. From 2014 to 2016, membership of the Scottish National Party (SNP) more than quadrupled. Rather than 'dealigning', the electorate has been 'realigninig' to a broader range of parties. Furthermore, Labour's membership soared from fewer than 190,000 in 2013 to more than 500,000 by 2021. It is clearly possible, then, for a major party to attract large numbers of members, which contradicts the notion that the electorate are 'dealigning'. In 2019, 1.7% of the electorate were members of a political party, compared to just 0.8% in 2013. While these figures have yet to return to the heights of 1983 (3.8%), the direction of travel suggests that any process of dealignment is over.
>
> Source: original material, 2021

Analyse, evaluate and compare the arguments in the above extract about partisan dealignment. [25]

3. 'The UK is a thriving representative democracy.' Analyse and evaluate this statement. [25]

Answers available online

7 Elections and referendums

Key points

- Britain uses the first-past-the-post (FPTP) electoral system in general elections, but it has significant weaknesses.
- Alternative voting systems are used in other elections across the UK, with mixed results.
- Voting behaviour in general elections is influenced by a wide range of different factors, as revealed by three election case studies.
- Referendums have been used more frequently since 1998, though debates continue as to their impact on democracy.

Electoral systems

First-past-the-post

- A plurality system in which the electorate votes for one candidate in their constituency.
- Whichever candidate gets the most votes, wins.
- Candidates do not need to win a majority of votes cast.
- Used in general elections in the UK to elect representatives (MPs) to the House of Commons.

Table 7.1 outlines the advantages and disadvantages of the FPTP system.

Table 7.1 The advantages and disadvantages of FPTP

	Advantages	Disadvantages
Voting	- Simple: voters put an X next to their preferred candidate. - Easy to understand: whoever gets the most votes, wins the seat.	- Millions of **wasted votes** nationally. - It encourages **tactical voting**. - The choice of candidate is made by the party, not the voter. If a voter wishes to vote Conservative, for example, they cannot choose between a selection of Conservative candidates. - Turnout tends to be lower in countries that use FPTP than in countries with proportional systems.
Constituencies	- Each constituency is represented by one MP, so constituents know whom to contact.	- A majority of voters in a constituency may have voted *against* their representative. - Voters in **safe seats** can feel that there is no point in voting if they do not support that party. - Election campaigns tend to ignore safe seats and focus instead on **marginal seats** (seats won by a margin of 5% or less of all votes). - In 2019, there were only 67 marginal seats, meaning that the vast majority of seats were uncompetitive. - Differing population sizes in constituencies mean that not all votes count equally: in 2019, the largest UK constituency was the Isle of Wight, with an electorate of 113,020; the smallest was Na h-Eileanan an Iar in Scotland, with an electorate of 21,106.

	Advantages	**Disadvantages**
Parties	+ FPTP tends to produce a two-party system, giving voters a clear choice between two broad parties, each of which has a realistic chance of forming a government. + Extremist parties find it difficult to win seats.	+ It favours parties with concentrated geographical support. + Minor parties win far fewer seats in the House of Commons than they would if seats were allocated proportionally to votes. In 2015, UKIP won just one seat for 3.9 million votes. + Minor parties struggle to convince supporters to vote for them, as their vote is likely to be wasted. + It is difficult for new parties to break into politics.
Governments	+ FPTP tends to result in majority single-party governments, which find it easier to pass legislation. + Majority governments have a clear mandate for their manifestos. + Governments are easily held accountable by the electorate for implementing their manifestos. + Coalitions and minority governments are rare (seen as a good thing as they are traditionally weaker and less stable than majority governments).	+ FPTP exaggerates the mandate that governments actually have. In 1997, Labour won 2.5 times as many seats as the Conservatives, but only 1.4 times as many votes. This is known as a 'winner's bonus'. + Since 2010, the rise of minor and regional parties (particularly the Scottish National Party (SNP) since 2015) has made it difficult for either the Conservatives or Labour to win a large majority. + In effect, the UK now has a multi-party system but a voting system designed for two parties. + It does not guarantee strong majority governments. From 2010 to 2015 the UK had a coalition government, and a minority government from 2017–19.

Wasted votes Votes that do not contribute to the election of a political candidate. This includes votes for losing candidates and those for a winning candidate that are in excess of the threshold required for them to win the seat.

Tactical voting When a voter does not vote for their preferred party because they do not believe that party can win. Instead, they vote for another party that has a better chance of winning. This may be to stop a party they dislike from winning.

Safe seats Those seats in which one party has such a large majority that it is highly unlikely it could be won by another party.

Marginal seats Those seats in which the MP's majority is small, meaning that it could easily be won by another party.

Making links

Those who argue that the UK has a participation crisis often blame FPTP. Advocates of electoral reform claim that safe seats and the need for tactical voting encourage political apathy and low turnout. A Best for Britain poll in 2021 found that two-fifths of people felt their vote had been wasted in recent FPTP elections.

Exam tip

Do not assume that the arguments against FPTP easily outweigh its benefits, as the reality is more complex. UK voters were offered the chance to change the voting system in the 2011 Alternative Vote referendum, but chose to keep FPTP. The main advantages of FPTP are its simplicity and the tendency to produce majority governments that the electorate can easily hold to account.

Now test yourself

TESTED

1 What type of electoral system is FPTP?
2 What are wasted votes?
3 What is a winner's bonus?
4 What is a safe seat?

Answers on p. 126

Majoritarian and proportional electoral systems

REVISED

- Majoritarian systems require a candidate to gain 50% plus one vote to win (an absolute majority). They are not proportional, so are likely to result in majority governments.
- Proportional systems allocate seats in proportion to the number of votes received by each party. They are likely to result in coalition governments.
- Mixed systems involve two types of representatives elected using different systems. Representatives of single-member constituencies are elected using a plurality or majoritarian system. Representatives of larger multi-member constituencies are elected using a proportional system. These systems are explained in more detail in Table 7.2.

Making links

The Liberal Democrats have long campaigned for the UK to use proportional representation instead of FPTP. The party has never had the concentrated geographical support needed to dominate in a FPTP system, despite its widespread popularity with voters across the country at various times in its history.

Table 7.2 Alternatives to FPTP

	Majoritarian	**Proportional**	**Mixed**
Electoral system	Supplementary Vote (SV)	Single Transferable Vote (STV)	Additional Member System (AMS)
Where used	Elections for the mayor of London, directly elected metro mayors (see p. 52), and police and crime commissioners	Northern Ireland Assembly elections and Scottish local council elections	Elections to the Scottish and Welsh Parliaments, and the London Assembly
Features	+ A candidate needs to gain 50% plus one vote to win (an absolute majority). + Single-member constituencies. + Voters choose a first and second preference candidate. + If no candidate wins a majority from the first preferences, the second preferences of all but the top two candidates are counted. + The second preferences are added to the first preferences for the top two candidates to produce a winner.	+ Proportional representation: seats are allocated in proportion to the number of votes received by each party. + Large multi-member constituencies. + Voters write numbers next to the candidates in order of their preference. + Candidates need a certain number of votes (the Droop quota) to win a seat. + Once a candidate meets the quota, their extra votes are reallocated to second preferences. + As candidates continue to meet the quota, remaining votes continue to be reallocated until all the seats are filled.	+ The greater proportion of seats in the legislature are elected using FPTP. + A smaller proportion of seats are allocated using proportional representation. + The FPTP seats represent single-member constituencies. + The regional list seats represent larger multimember constituencies. + The proportion of each party's share of the vote in the regional list vote is calculated, and compared against the proportion of votes it has won in the FPTP vote. If it has a lower proportion of FPTP seats than it deserves, it is allocated additional member seats from the regional list to 'top up' its share of seats.

	Majoritarian	**Proportional**	**Mixed**
Advantages	+ Increased legitimacy: representatives need to command broader support than under FPTP. + Choice: voters can vote for minor parties with their first preference and use their second preference for whichever front-runner they would most like to win.	+ Proportional: voters can support minor parties knowing their vote will count. + Greatest choice: using STV, voters can choose both the party and the individual candidate.	+ Much more proportional than FPTP or majoritarian systems. + Choice: voters can confidently vote for minor parties with their regional list vote. + Split-ticket voting allows voters to choose one party for their constituency vote, and a different party for their list vote. + Constituency seats retain the relationship between the MP and their constituency.
Disadvantages	+ Not proportional. + Very difficult for minor parties to win, although they may receive support at the first preference stage. + Votes for anyone other than the two main candidates are still wasted. + Despite being a majoritarian system, it is possible for the winner to be elected without a majority. + Can result in the election of the 'least-worst' candidate rather than the best (the ultimate winner may not have won the first preference vote).	+ Coalition governments are highly likely: these may be weak or unstable. + Constituencies: the link between the voter and their representative is weaker as the constituencies are so large and have several different representatives. + Complex counting system. + Complex voting process: voters may find it difficult or confusing if they lack the knowledge to choose between different parties *and* candidates.	+ A hybrid system, so not perfectly proportional. + Two classes of representative are elected: some represent constituencies, others larger regions. + Voters cannot choose between individual candidates on the closed list, just between parties. + Majority governments are less likely than with FPTP. + Relatively complex voting system: the voter makes two choices and needs to understand two voting systems.

> **Regional list** A proportional system in which seats are allocated from votes using the d'Hondt formula. A closed list system is used: parties rank their candidates in the order that they will be elected and voters simply choose a party. Regional lists were used in UK elections to the European Parliament before the UK left the EU in 2020.

Impact of electoral systems on the party system

REVISED

+ FPTP tends to produce a two-party system, with a single party forming a majority government.
+ In recent years, voters' growing support for minor and regional parties has led to a coalition government (2010–15 Conservatives and Liberal Democrats) and a minority government (2017–19 Conservative government with a confidence and supply agreement with the Democratic Unionist Party), despite the use of FPTP.
+ Minor parties thrived when proportional representation was used; for example, in the European Parliament elections, the Brexit Party won in 2019 with the Liberal Democrats in second place, and UKIP won in 2014.
+ Some argue that the UK is now in effect a multi-party system that would benefit from a different electoral system in general elections.
+ Majoritarian systems such as SV tend to produce a two-party system. They make it harder for more extreme minor parties to win seats than under FPTP, as they need a majority of votes. It is easier for centrist minor parties (e.g. the Liberal Democrats) to win seats, as they are more likely to be a second preference.

> **Exam tip**
>
> Do not assume that *any* alternative to FPTP will benefit minor parties: this is not the case. Proportional systems will increase the representation of smaller parties, but majoritarian systems will not. This is because minor parties find it difficult to win a majority of the vote unless their supporters are geographically concentrated (as in the case of the Scottish National Party).

+ Proportional systems such as STV usually result in a multi-party system with coalition governments.
+ STV has worked effectively in the Northern Ireland Assembly, where the long history of conflict between nationalists and unionists makes it essential that seats accurately reflect votes cast. A power-sharing agreement means that the government is run by both nationalists and unionists.
+ The mixed system AMS has allowed a multi-party system to emerge in Scotland. Coalition or minority governments are the most likely outcome of a Scottish Parliament election, but it is still possible for a party to form a majority government: the SNP did so in 2011.
+ The regional list element of AMS allowed the SNP to become the second-biggest party in the first Scottish Parliament in 1999, despite its lack of concentrated support. The SNP won the 2007 election and formed its first (minority) government. Since 2015 the party has also dominated in FPTP general elections, because it developed concentrated support across much of the country following its 2014 referendum campaign.

> **Making links**
>
> The SNP's majority win in the 2011 Scottish Parliament elections put pressure on the UK coalition government to allow an independence referendum. Although the SNP lost the referendum, their campaign quadrupled their membership numbers and allowed them to develop concentrated support across much of Scotland.
>
> The introduction of different voting systems in devolved elections since 1998 has changed the fortunes of minor parties across the UK and shaped the party system. As of 2022, a different party was in government in each of the four nations of the UK. You can learn more about the UK's development towards a multi-party system in Chapter 8.

> **Now test yourself** TESTED
>
> 5 What is a majoritarian system?
> 6 What type of system is STV?
> 7 Where is the SV system used in the UK?
> 8 What impact do proportional systems have on the party system?
>
> **Answers on p. 126**

> **Revision activity**
>
> 1 Write down as many advantages and disadvantages of the following as you can from memory:
>   + FPTP
>   + majoritarian systems
>   + proportional systems.
> 2 Check your answers against the information in this section and add in any missing points.
> 3 Decide which are the strongest and weakest arguments in favour of each voting system.

> **Exam tip**
>
> It can be difficult to remember all of the different voting systems: the best way is to develop your own opinion about which systems are best for democracy. This will also help you to analyse the electoral systems in the exam.

> **Exam tip**
>
> Students often waste too much time explaining *how* the different voting systems work, rather than analysing their *impact*. As a general rule, avoid writing more than a sentence of explanation for each system.

Voting behaviour

Voting behaviour describes how people tend to vote. The study of voting behaviour includes looking at patterns of *how* people vote and analysis of *why* they vote that way.

Factors influencing voting behaviour

REVISED

Age

+ In 2017 and 2019, age was the most important predictor of how people voted in the general election.
+ Young people were more likely to vote Labour in 2019 than older people (over the age of 39), who were more likely to vote Conservative.
+ In the 2016 EU referendum, a majority of 18- to 34-year-olds of every social class voted to remain, whereas a majority of over-55s in each social class voted to leave (Ipsos MORI survey).
+ Turnout increases with age: fewer than 55% of 18- to 24-year-olds voted in the 2019 general election, compared to more than 80% of those aged 75 years or more.

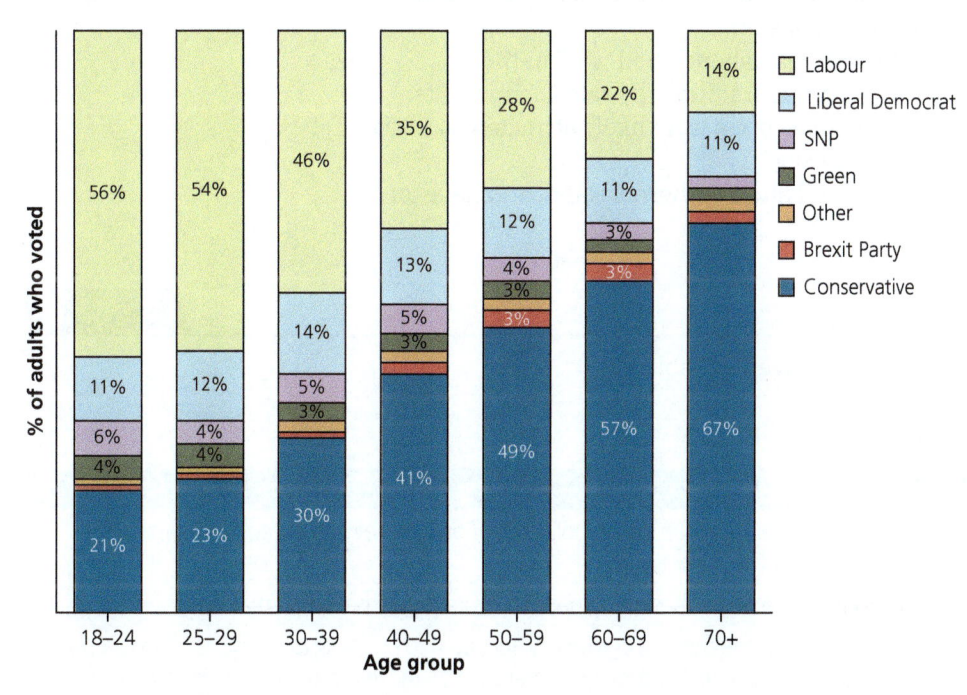

Figure 7.1 Age distribution of voting behaviour in the 2019 general election

Class

+ Traditionally, class was the main predictor of how people would vote: working-class voters were more likely to support Labour, whereas middle-class voters were more likely to support the Conservatives.
+ Since the 1980s, the process of class dealignment has meant that class is less important in determining voting behaviour. It can still be relevant, however: in the 2016 EU referendum, middle-class voters were more likely to vote to remain than working-class voters of the same age.
+ In the 2019 general election, voters of all classes were more likely to vote Conservative than Labour, with skilled manual workers more likely to vote Conservative than any other social class.
+ Education level was closely linked to voting behaviour in 2019: voters who had a degree-level education or above were far more likely to vote Labour, while all other voters were more likely to vote Conservative.

> **Exam tip**
>
> Do not assume that class is the most important factor in determining voting behaviour; this is no longer true. Age, education and geography are now much more reliable predictors of how people vote.

Gender

- Men and women may have different priorities: some believe that women are more likely to support parties that favour strong public services, particularly the NHS and education.
- Women were more likely to vote to remain in the EU than men.
- Women and men are equally likely to turn out to vote.
- There was a very small gender gap in the 2019 election: women were slightly more likely to vote Labour than men. However, among young people (18–24 years) this gender gap was much more pronounced.

Ethnicity

- Black, Asian and minority ethnic (BAME) groups are significantly more likely to vote Labour than Conservative: in 2019, an estimated 64% of BAME voters chose Labour.

Geography

- Rural English areas and southern constituencies are more likely to be Conservative.
- Urban areas, particularly in London and the North, are more likely to be held by Labour, as is much of south Wales.
- In 2019 the Conservatives broke through Labour's 'red wall' in the Midlands, the North and Wales, winning traditionally safe Labour seats. These seats had voted leave in 2016, so voters were likely attracted by Boris Johnson's 2019 pledge to 'Get Brexit Done'.
- Regional parties dominate in Scotland and Northern Ireland, and have an important presence in Wales.

Voter choice

REVISED

A number of theories of voter choice are given in Table 7.3.

Table 7.3 Theories of voter choice

Theory	Key features
Rational choice theory	Assumes that voters weigh up all the political options logically and vote for the party that will deliver the best result for them.
Issue voting	Voters prioritise one issue above all others and vote purely based on that issue.
Valence issues	Valence issues are those that are universally accepted to be important. Voters choose a party based on how well they think the party will perform on those issues. The economy is probably the most important valence issue. Other valence issues include healthcare and education.

> **Exam tip**
>
> Do not confuse issue voting and rational choice voting. People may be so committed to a single issue that they vote *against* what might be seen as their own best interests. For example, imagine a business owner who exported goods to the EU but prioritised reducing immigration above all else. They might well have voted leave in the 2016 EU referendum, despite the likely negative impact on their business.

> **Now test yourself** TESTED
>
> 9 Which factor was traditionally most important in explaining voting behaviour?
> 10 Which factor was the most important predictor of voting behaviour in the 2019 general election?
> 11 Which party are BAME voters most likely to support?
> 12 In which geographical regions do the Conservatives dominate most?
>
> Answers on p. 126

Election case studies

REVISED

Case study

The 1979 general election

Political context	+ Followed the 1978–9 'Winter of Discontent' strikes + Labour leader James Callaghan faced new Conservative leader Margaret Thatcher
Result	+ Conservative win + 43-seat majority
Patterns of voting behaviour	+ Middle class more likely to vote Conservative, working class more likely to vote Labour + All ages more likely to vote Conservative, apart from 18- to 24-year-olds + Women slightly more likely to vote Conservative than Labour, men equally likely + No records for BAME voters
Influence of the media	+ More media focus on leaders than previously + Thatcher used television photo opportunities to raise her profile + *The Sun* newspaper switched support from Labour to the Conservatives for the first time
Impact of party policies and manifestos	+ The Conservatives focused on getting the economy going again, lowering unemployment and preventing strike disruption + Conservative tax cuts and the Right to Buy scheme (giving council tenants the right to buy their council house at a heavily discounted price) were popular with voters
Impact of campaigns and leadership	+ Successful 'Labour isn't working' **campaign** by Conservatives focused on high unemployment + Thatcher was relatively unknown compared to Callaghan; some voters found her off-putting + British voters had no model for what a female prime minister would look and sound like
Impact of election on policy and policy making	+ Thatcher's majority allowed her to begin transforming Britain by privatising public industries, reducing union strikes and adopting a **monetarist economic policy** (which led to unemployment doubling by 1983) + Thatcher's policies became even bolder after she won a landslide in 1983

Campaign An attempt by a political party to persuade people to vote for its candidates or, in the case of a referendum, in accordance with its views.

Monetarist economic policy Economic policy that aims to keep inflation low by controlling the supply of money.

Case study

The 1997 general election

Political context	+ The Conservatives had been in power since 1979 and Prime Minister John Major's government was tainted by sleaze (financial and sex scandals) + Labour had moved to the centre politically since Tony Blair became leader in 1994
Result	+ Labour landslide + 179-seat majority + Best post-war result of any party + Best result ever for Labour
Patterns of voting behaviour	+ Labour made big gains among the middle class and skilled working class + All ages more likely to vote Labour, apart from the over-65s + Women and men equally likely to support Labour + 70% of BAME voters supported Labour, compared to 43% of white voters
Influence of the media	+ **New Labour** had a proactive approach to the media that was new to UK politics + Tony Blair went to Australia after becoming leader to meet Rupert Murdoch, owner of *The Sun* + *The Sun* switched support from the Conservatives to Labour + **Spin doctors** managed Labour's interactions with the media to ensure that daily stories kept coverage 'on message'

7 Elections and referendums

73

My Revision Notes AQA A-level UK Politics Second Edition

Impact of party policies and manifestos	+ Labour had centrist economic policies + The **Third Way** was designed to appeal to a broad range of voters + Labour made five pledges: to cut class sizes, to introduce fast-track punishments for persistent young offenders, to cut NHS waiting lists, to get under-25-year-olds into work, and not to raise income tax + The Conservatives were divided over Europe and very critical of Blair's devolution plans, neither of which impressed the electorate
Impact of campaigns and leadership	+ Negative campaigning from the Conservatives, with 'New Labour, New Danger' slogan + The Labour slogan promised change: 'Because Britain deserves better' + Campaigns focused on party leaders + At 43, Blair was younger than any prime minister since 1812 and lacked experience. However, his charisma and enthusiasm appealed to voters, as did his 1995 amendment of **Clause IV** of Labour's constitution
Impact of election on policy and policy making	+ Blair's huge majority allowed him to implement a wide range of policies including devolution, the removal of hereditary peers from the House of Lords, the passing of the Human Rights Act 1998 and the Freedom of Information Act 2000, the introduction of a national minimum wage and increased public spending

New Labour The policies and values introduced by Tony Blair after he became leader in 1994, which dominated until Ed Miliband became leader in 2010. New Labour accepted the capitalist economic system and focused on equality of opportunity rather than equality of outcome (giving people equal opportunities, but not an equal standard of living). New Labour was a 'catch-all' party with broad appeal to different social classes, including the middle class.

Spin doctors Political operatives who shape a politician's message so that it attracts maximum positive publicity. Blair's New Labour was famous for its use of spin doctors: the best-known were Alastair Campbell and Peter Mandelson.

Third Way An ideological compromise developed by Blair's New Labour. It was a balance between centre-right economic policy and centre-left social policy, which focused on social justice rather than a socialist restructuring of the economic system.

Clause IV Part of the 1918 Labour constitution, which committed Labour to the 'common ownership of the means of production, distribution and exchange', meaning widespread nationalisation. In 1995 Blair rewrote the clause, removing references to socialist economic policy.

Case study

The 2019 general election

Political context	+ Boris Johnson had been prime minister since July 2019, and called a **snap election** for December + The Conservatives were a minority government and deeply divided. Theresa May had resigned as leader earlier that year after failing to unite parliament behind her Brexit deal, and Johnson faced the same problem + To trigger a snap election to break the impasse, Johnson convinced parliament to pass the Early Parliamentary General Election Act 2019 (this bypassed the Fixed-term Parliaments Act 2011) + The last three elections (2010, 2015 and 2017) had been very close, so many people expected the 2019 result would be too
Result	+ Overwhelming Conservative victory: 80-seat majority, taking 54 seats from Labour + Labour had its worst election result since 1935, forcing the resignation of leader Jeremy Corbyn + Regional parties continued to perform well: the SNP won 48 seats in Scotland (taking 7 from the Conservatives); Sinn Féin and the Democratic Unionist Party continued to dominate in Northern Ireland

Check your understanding and progress at www.hoddereducation.co.uk/myrevisionnotesdownloads

Patterns of voting behaviour	+ Older people (over 39 years old), homeowners and all social classes were more likely to vote Conservative + Young people, BAME voters, home renters, those with a degree-level education or higher were all more likely to vote Labour + Conservatives broke through Labour's 'red wall', winning 24 previously safe Labour seats in the Midlands, the North and Wales
Influence of the media	+ Right-wing newspapers *The Sun*, the *Daily Mail* and the *Express* supported the Conservatives + Social media spending was concentrated on Facebook (now Meta) and YouTube; Labour outspent the Conservatives (£4 million on social media compared to £900,000), which perhaps partly explains their success with younger voters + Johnson was criticised for refusing to be interviewed one-on-one by broadcaster Andrew Neil, and for avoiding a Channel 4 debate on climate change, but this did not stop him winning the election + The Conservatives and Labour managed to exclude other parties from the main television leadership debate, emphasising the idea of a two-horse race
Impact of party policies and manifestos	+ The Conservatives' focus on achieving Brexit was popular after three years of gridlock; they promised 50,000 new nurses, money for social care and the police, without raising income tax, VAT or national insurance, and pledged the UK would be carbon neutral by 2050 + Labour offered a more confusing position on Brexit: a renegotiated deal followed by a second referendum. Other policies included increased spending on the NHS and a rise in the national minimum wage, pledging the UK would be carbon neutral by 2030 + The Liberal Democrats promised to rejoin the EU without a second referendum if they won a majority, which was criticised as an undemocratic rejection of the 2016 referendum; party leader Jo Swinson lost her seat in the election
Impact of campaigns and leadership	+ Johnson's relentless repetition of his slogan 'Get Brexit Done' was highly effective; populist policies helped him to extend his appeal to working-class 'red wall' voters + Jeremy Corbyn's leadership was seen as a weakness, and as lacking appeal to working-class voters, despite his relative success in the 2017 general election (in which Labour prevented the Tories from winning a majority); accusations of anti-Semitism within the party also damaged his image + Labour's Brexit position was much criticised — Labour was torn between its leave-voting 'red wall' seats and remain-voting London seats, and it was impossible for the party to satisfy both
Impact of election on policy and policy making	+ Johnson 'got Brexit done' in January 2020, when the UK left the EU + Johnson began a 'levelling up' agenda with the aim of keeping former Labour seats in Conservative hands; the government promised to reduce economic inequalities across the UK through investment and increasing skills through apprenticeships + The 2020 coronavirus pandemic transformed government policy, forcing the highest levels of borrowing since the Second World War, a national furlough scheme, the introduction of national restrictions and three periods of enforced lockdown + Johnson's healthy majority helped him to ignore calls for an emergency coalition government

> **Exam tip**
>
> The best answers use examples to support their analysis, so learn the details of these case studies and try to apply them to different questions on elections. You may also be asked to refer specifically to case studies, depending on the question. You are expected to understand one election before 1997, the 1997 general election itself and one election after 1997.

> **Revision activity**
>
> 1 Using the three case studies given here, make a list of the main factors that influenced the outcome of each election.
> 2 For each election, decide which was the most important factor.

Snap election A general election that is held earlier than expected and typically occurs relatively quickly after being announced. A government may seek a snap election if it believes it can win a big majority. The Fixed-term Parliaments Act 2011 states that general elections should happen every five years, but a government can still trigger a snap election if at least two-thirds of MPs vote for it.

Examples of particular characteristics of the British electoral system

Table 7.4 characterises a selection of British general elections.

> **Disenfranchised** When someone's right to vote has been removed.

Table 7.4 Examples of characteristics of British general elections

A landslide victory for one party	**1997 (Labour)** + The biggest landslide victory since the Second World War
A clear discrepancy between the number of votes and the number of seats gained	**2015 (Conservative)** + UKIP won 3.9 million votes but gained just one seat in the House of Commons + The Greens won 1.1 million votes and also won one seat + The contrast between UKIP and the SNP's result was even more startling: the SNP was rewarded with 56 MPs for just 1.5 million votes
Large numbers of voters being effectively **disenfranchised** by the preponderance of voters for one party in large areas of the country	**2015 (Conservative)** + The SNP won a landslide victory in Scotland, winning 56 of 59 seats; for the first time in its history, it became the third-largest party in the UK Parliament + 1.5 million Scots voted for the SNP, nearly 50% of the popular vote + This means that just over 50% of the Scottish popular vote went *against* the SNP, yet it received 95% of Scottish seats in the House of Commons + Scottish voters who did not support the SNP might claim to be effectively disenfranchised as their votes did not translate into representation in the Commons
An election in which the outcome was greatly influenced by a particular leadership style or personality	**1997 (Labour)** + Tony Blair's leadership was crucial to Labour's landslide win + He was young, charismatic and a skilled communicator; he used spin doctors to manipulate the media and convinced Rupert Murdoch of *The Sun* to support him + He had the vision and leadership to create New Labour, moving the party to the centre of the political spectrum and reassuring many middle-class voters that Labour could be trusted with the economy **2017 (Conservative)** + Having chosen to fight an election based on her own 'strong and stable' leadership abilities, Theresa May failed to connect with voters + May lost her majority after a campaign criticised for political mistakes, misjudged policies, her aloof personal style, and her refusal to appear in the main televised debates + In contrast, Jeremy Corbyn's popularity surged, particularly with younger voters; opinion polling on the two leaders reversed during the campaign, which May had begun with a huge lead

> **Now test yourself** TESTED
>
> 13 What slogan did the Conservatives use to criticise Labour during the 1979 election?
> 14 Why was the 1997 election historic?
> 15 Why did UKIP's 2015 election result demonstrate a major problem with FPTP?
> 16 What issue was the main focus of the 2019 election?
>
> Answers on p. 126

> **Exam tip**
>
> You need to have examples for the different scenarios listed in Table 7.4, so make sure you learn them in detail.

Referendums

Referendum rules and procedures

+ There is no legal requirement for most referendums to be held. However, the Scotland Act 2016 and Wales Act 2017 forbid the abolition of the Scottish or Welsh Parliaments without a referendum.
+ It has become a constitutional convention that referendums will be called for significant constitutional change, such as the referendums on AV (2011), Scottish independence (2014) and membership of the EU (2016).

+ The government can set any referendum question, but the Electoral Commission comments on proposed questions. The government is likely to take their advice.
+ Any group or individual spending over £10,000 campaigning during a referendum has to submit a return to the Electoral Commission and must keep to a spending limit.
+ The Electoral Commission oversees the conduct of the referendum and writes a report afterwards.
+ The result of the referendum is not legally binding. Parliament is still sovereign so the government can, in theory, ignore the result, although in practice this would be profoundly undemocratic.

A number of reasons for calling referendums are given in Table 7.5.

Table 7.5 Reasons for calling referendums

Reason	Significance
Constitutional change	To give a specific mandate for planned constitutional change, e.g. the devolution of Scotland and Wales in 1997.
Political forces	Governments may feel compelled to call a referendum if nationalist parties are gaining ground, e.g. the 2014 Scottish independence referendum and the 2016 EU referendum.
Party or government management	To settle an issue: prime ministers may hold a referendum on an issue that is dividing their party or government. This happened in 1975 when the Labour government was divided over remaining in the EEC, and in 2011 when the Conservative–Liberal Democrat coalition government held a referendum on changing the voting system, which the Liberal Democrats supported but the Conservatives did not.
The Localism Act 2011	This Act was intended to devolve power to local governments, including an increase in local referendums. Local referendums must be called on certain plans for housing development and to increase council tax above levels set by central government. The majority of referendums on the introduction of directly elected mayors resulted in a 'no' vote but, as of 2021, there were 15 directly elected mayors in England (in addition to the Mayor of London and nine 'metro mayors').

UK referendums

REVISED

Table 7.6 outlines the main referendums held in the UK since 1975.

Table 7.6 UK referendums since 1975

Referendum	Context	Result	Impact
UK European Communities membership referendum, 1975	Labour Prime Minister Harold Wilson called this referendum because his party and cabinet were split over Europe	67% of the electorate voted to stay in the EEC	Britain remained in the EEC, which later developed into the European Union (EU)
Scottish devolution referendum, 1979 Welsh devolution referendum, 1979	Growing calls for devolution	Scotland voted to have its own assembly (parliament), but did not meet the 40% **threshold** set by the government Wales voted against an assembly	Devolution did not happen Scottish nationalists were hugely frustrated that the vote did not meet the threshold
Scottish devolution referendum, 1997 Welsh devolution referendum, 1997	Tony Blair used referendums to legitimise his constitutional changes He introduced a Scottish Parliament and a Welsh Assembly	Scotland voted 'yes' by 74% to 25% In Wales the result was more ambiguous: with only a 50% turnout, 50.3% voted 'yes' to 49.7% 'no'	The Scottish Parliament and Welsh Assembly were set up Each was given devolved powers
Greater London Authority referendum, 1998	Part of Blair's devolution programme	A clear majority voted 'yes' (72%) A low turnout of 34% was a poor mandate for local devolution	London gained its own assembly and a directly elected mayor

My Revision Notes AQA A-level UK Politics Second Edition

7 Elections and referendums

Referendum	Context	Result	Impact
Northern Ireland Good Friday Agreement referendum, 1998	A landmark moment in UK history The people of Northern Ireland were asked to support the peace agreement that aimed to end the Troubles (see p. 51)	71% of voters supported the agreement A high turnout of 81% gave the agreement crucial legitimacy	A devolved assembly was set up A power-sharing agreement gave both nationalists and unionists a role in government STV is used for assembly elections, ensuring the sensitive mix of political opinion in Northern Ireland is accurately reflected
North East England devolution referendum, 2004	Blair's Labour government planned to extend devolution to the regions of the UK by introducing regional assemblies, starting with the northeast of England	78% of voters in the northeast rejected the plan A low turnout of 48% also suggested that this referendum had not sparked much public interest	The government was surprised and disappointed This referendum effectively ended government plans to introduce regional devolution
Welsh devolution referendum, 2011	Plaid Cymru and Welsh Labour both wanted to increase Wales's law-making powers	Wales voted 'yes' (63%) A very low turnout of 35.6%	Wales received greater law-making powers
UK Alternative Vote referendum, 2011	The coalition agreement included a referendum on AV as a compromise: the Conservatives wanted to keep FPTP, whereas the Lib Dems wanted proportional representation The public struggled to understand the complexities of the AV system and the campaigns failed to inspire	68% voted to keep FPTP Only 42% of the electorate turned out	FPTP continues to be used for UK general elections The low turnout and emphatic rejection of AV makes it unlikely that any political party will attempt to change the voting system again for many years
Scottish independence referendum, 2014	Prime Minister David Cameron was criticised by some Conservatives for calling this referendum as it risked the break-up of the UK Cameron argued that he had no choice: the SNP had won a majority in the 2011 Scottish Parliament elections with an independence referendum in their manifesto The SNP campaigned for 'Yes Scotland' while the Tories, Lib Dems and Labour ran 'Better together'	55% of voters chose to remain in the UK There was a record turnout of 84.5% The campaigns saw huge political participation across Scotland 16- and 17-year-olds were allowed to vote	Scotland remained in the UK Following the 2016 EU referendum (in which Scotland voted to remain), the Scottish government, led by SNP leader Nicola Sturgeon, pushed for a second Scottish independence referendum After losing seats in the 2017 election, Sturgeon decided to wait until Brexit was finished, as her focus on a second referendum may have contributed to the SNP's weaker result
UK European Union membership referendum, 2016	In their 2015 manifesto, the Conservatives promised an EU referendum Cameron included the referendum to stop Tory voters from switching to UKIP and to placate **Eurosceptics** in his party	52% voted to leave, 48% to remain Turnout was high, at 72%	Cameron resigned: he had taken a massive political gamble, but it had failed Theresa May became prime minister, but was unable to lead Britain through the Brexit process

Check your understanding and progress at www.hoddereducation.co.uk/myrevisionnotesdownloads

Referendum	Context	Result	Impact
	The campaigns were cross-party. Tories Boris Johnson and Michael Gove headed the 'Vote Leave' campaign with Labour MP Gisela Stuart. UKIP ran a separate Leave campaign Cameron and most government ministers campaigned for 'Remain', along with much of Labour and all Liberal Democrats The Leave campaigns were criticised for inaccurate claims, while Remain focused on economic risks and failed to give positive reasons to stay		The British public seemed divided as never before The referendum result put parliament (where a majority wished to remain) at odds with a majority of the people In 2017 MPs voted to begin the process of leaving the EU but were unable to agree on a Brexit deal, even after pro-leave Johnson became prime minister The 2019 election was needed to give Johnson a clear mandate for Brexit: the UK finally left the EU in 2020

Threshold The minimum proportion of the electorate who need to vote 'yes' in a referendum in order for their decision to be implemented. The government decides whether to set a threshold. A threshold is not generally used in the UK, but the most notable exception was the 1979 Scottish devolution referendum.

Eurosceptics Those who do not support the increasing powers of the EU and are suspicious and critical of it.

Making links

Brexit put huge pressure on the integrity of the UK.
- Scotland voted to remain (62%), and the SNP accordingly demanded a second independence referendum.
- Northern Ireland also voted to remain and its ongoing relationship with Ireland (an EU member) and the rest of the UK proved to be a major sticking point in the Brexit negotiations. The final deal aligned Northern Ireland to the EU's common market, avoiding a hard border with Ireland but requiring checks on certain goods coming in from the rest of the UK. Unionists in Northern Ireland were deeply opposed, and some commentators warned of a threat to peace.

Revision activity

Make a list of different types of referendums, adding all the referendums in Table 7.6 as examples:
- national referendums
- devolved nations only (Scotland, Wales and Northern Ireland)
- regional referendums
- local referendums.

Impact of referendums on democracy

REVISED

Table 7.7 gives a number of positive and negative impacts of referendums on democracy.

Table 7.7 Positive and negative impacts of referendums

Positive	Negative
- Referendums have enhanced direct democracy, telling politicians what the electorate thinks more accurately than any opinion poll - High turnout in some referendums is evidence of improved political participation - Referendums give legitimacy to important decisions - The regular use of referendums since 1998 suggests that they have been an effective means of decision making - The electorate has surprised the government on several occasions, causing shifts in policy that would otherwise not have happened	- Governments still hold the power, not the people: governments tend not to hold referendums that they think they might lose - Low turnout in some referendums suggests that the public are not always engaged - Referendums can threaten parliamentary sovereignty and representative democracy - Poor-quality campaigns can mislead or confuse the public - Referendums offer no protection against the tyranny of the majority (when the majority of people may vote for something that undermines the rights of a minority group)

My Revision Notes AQA A-level UK Politics Second Edition

Making links

Referendums are an example of direct democracy. Sometimes, this can conflict with representative democracy, as happened with Brexit. The people voted to leave but parliament is sovereign so had the final say, and most MPs were pro-remain. While many felt duty-bound to honour the wishes of the people, MPs could not agree on a Brexit deal until the 2019 election produced a parliament that better reflected the referendum result.

Exam skills

The elections and referendums topic requires you to master a large range of detailed information. There are four main areas to focus on:
+ electoral systems
+ voting behaviour
+ the three election case studies
+ referendums.

Within each topic, you need to cover all aspects on the specification, which have been included in this chapter. The most common mistake that students make when revising is to learn the features of the different types of electoral systems, but not their *impact* on parties and the party system in the UK.

You need to understand how the fortunes of the Conservatives, Labour, the Liberal Democrats, the Scottish Nationalist Party, and minor parties have been affected by the electoral systems in place in different regions of the UK and in different elections. Be aware that Northern Ireland's complex history and peace process means that it is essential for the country to have an electoral system that accurately reflects the democratic wishes of its people (STV).

Exam tip

If you are asked about the impact of referendums, make sure you use specific, recent examples. This tells the examiner that you are fully up to date. They would think it strange if you did not mention the 2016 EU referendum at all.

Now test yourself   TESTED

17 How many national referendums have there been?
18 In which circumstance has calling a referendum become a convention?
19 Which referendum in the UK had the highest turnout?
20 Why did the 2016 EU referendum challenge representative democracy?

Answers on p. 126

Summary

You should now have an understanding of:
+ the FPTP electoral system and its advantages and disadvantages
+ majoritarian and proportional electoral systems, their advantages and disadvantages, and their impact on the party system
+ the factors influencing voting behaviour
+ three general election case studies — 1979, 1997 and 2019 — and patterns of voting behaviour in those elections
+ the influence and impact of the media, party policies, manifestos, campaigns and leadership in the three election case studies, and their impact on policy and policy making
+ examples of particular characteristics of British elections
+ the nature and use of referendums in the UK and their impact.

Exam practice

1. Explain and analyse three features of the FPTP voting system. [9]
2. 'The use of referendums since 1998 has strengthened UK democracy.' Analyse and evaluate this statement. [25]
3. 'Party leadership is the most important factor in determining the outcome of UK general elections.' Analyse and evaluate this statement, with reference to one pre-1997 election, the 1997 election and one post-1997 election. [25]

Answers available online

8 Political parties

Key points

REVISED

- The UK has a wide variety of political parties, with a diverse range of ideas and policies.
- The extent to which ordinary members are able to participate in decision making varies between the Conservatives, Labour and the Liberal Democrats.
- Party funding is a controversial issue, particularly given the impact of wealthy donors.
- Political parties win elections because of many different factors, one of which is their relationship with the media.
- Minor parties play an increasingly important role in UK politics, leading some to argue that the UK now has a multi-party system.

Origins, ideas and development

Conservatives

REVISED

Table 8.1 outlines the origins, ideas and development of the Conservative Party.

Table 8.1 The Conservative Party

Origins	<ul><li>Dates back to 1834.</li><li>Traditionally the party represented the wealthy.</li><li>Benjamin Disraeli (leader 1868–81) developed **one-nation conservatism** to attract support from the first working-class voters.</li><li>Once universal suffrage was introduced in Britain in 1928, the party further reinvented itself with policies that appealed to an even broader range of supporters.</li><li>Dominated UK politics in the twentieth century, with 67 years in office.</li></ul>
Ideas	<ul><li>One-nation conservatism dominated before 1979.</li><li>**Thatcherism** was a much more radical, **neo-liberal** version of conservatism. It was part of the New Right movement that included US president Ronald Reagan. Thatcher maintained traditional conservative social values.</li><li>'Compassionate conservatism' was adopted by David Cameron: it combined Thatcherite free-market economic policies with more liberal social values and concern for society and the environment. However, austerity and cuts to public spending defined his government's response to the 2008 financial crisis.</li><li>There have been many battles between Eurosceptics and **Europhiles**: even after the 2016 Brexit vote, the party was divided between Brexiteers and Remainers until Boris Johnson won a majority in 2019.</li><li>Johnson's 'levelling up' agenda aimed to reduce economic inequalities across the UK through investment and increasing skills through apprenticeships. Many saw this, and his government's response to the pandemic, as a form of one-nation conservatism.</li><li>Traditional conservative values were evident in the Johnson government's so-called 'war on woke'. For example, Home Secretary Priti Patel dismissed taking the knee against racism as 'gesture politics'.</li></ul>
Development	<ul><li>Conservatives accepted the **post-war consensus** before Margaret Thatcher became leader.</li><li>Thatcher (leader 1975–90) was impatient with her party's tolerance of high taxation, powerful and disruptive unions, and economic stagnation. She moved the UK sharply to the right when she became prime minister in 1979.</li><li>Thatcher adopted a confident foreign policy: protecting one of the UK's overseas territories in the 1982 Falklands War, playing a leading role alongside Ronald Reagan in Cold War diplomacy and winning a financial rebate from the European Community (which later became the EU).</li></ul>

- Thatcher's successor, John Major, largely continued Thatcherite policies. The struggles within the party over Europe intensified during his leadership.
- The party passed through the political wilderness during the New Labour era. David Cameron aimed to detoxify its image when he became leader in 2005.
- The Conservatives won the most seats in 2010 and formed a coalition with the Liberal Democrats. Their support allowed Cameron to legalise same-sex marriage in 2013, (which most of his own MPs opposed), but the coalition was defined by its controversial austerity policies. In 2015 Cameron won a small majority.
- Cameron's decision to hold a referendum on Britain's EU membership backfired for him: he failed to convince the public to remain, and resigned.
- Theresa May's 2017 manifesto supported grammar schools, bringing back fox hunting and the removal of universal free school lunches for 4- to 7-year-olds, suggesting a move away from Cameron's modern conservatism.
- May's failure to win a majority left her dependent on the Democratic Unionist Party (DUP) and unable to develop her own version of conservatism. The party was consumed by Brexit divisions.
- Johnson's 2019 election victory was a victory for Leavers within the party. His **populist** promises included more nurses and police officers, an Australian-style points system to tackle immigration, and a commitment not to raise income tax, VAT or national insurance.
- The 2020 coronavirus pandemic forced Johnson to overturn decades of Conservative policy and dramatically expand the role of the state. The furlough scheme and other economic support measures required the highest levels of government spending since the Second World War.
- Johnson's government introduced the greatest peacetime restrictions on individual liberty, including three national lockdowns and heavy fines for refusal to self-isolate. This was strongly opposed by some libertarians within the Conservative Party, though most Conservative MPs accepted the need to protect public health at the temporary expense of individual freedom.

One-nation conservatism A version of conservatism that includes policies designed to benefit all sections of society.

Thatcherism Margaret Thatcher's distinctive brand of conservatism. It included a monetarist economic policy (see p. 73), deregulation of business and finance, privatisation of industry and restriction of trade union powers.

Neo-liberal A liberal **ideology** that promotes free-market capitalism.

Ideology Core political beliefs and ideas, e.g. liberalism, conservatism, socialism.

Europhiles Those who support the EU project and see the EU as a force for good.

Post-war consensus The acceptance by both of the main political parties that Britain should retain the post-war settlement (the nationalised industries and generous welfare state first introduced by the 1945 Labour government).

Populist A politician who presents themselves as the true champion of ordinary people, defending their interests against the political elite.

Making links

Many of Johnson's policies, particularly his 'levelling up' agenda (which aims to reduce regional inequalities in the UK by helping communities that feel they have been 'left behind') were intended to appeal to working-class voters. The Conservatives particularly want to please voters in the former 'red wall' seats in the Midlands, North and Wales that they won in 2019. You can learn more about the 2019 general election in Chapter 7.

Conservatism is a very successful ideology, partly because of its pragmatism, which allows it to adapt to different time periods and contexts. The Conservatives spent more than 60 years in government over the course of the twentieth century, and have been in power since 2010 (including five years of coalition).

Exam tip

Remember that not all Conservatives oppose change: Thatcher introduced sweeping changes to Britain. However, her reforms had a conservative basis as her aim was to return Britain to its 'former glory'.

> **Now test yourself** TESTED
>
> 1 Give three features of Thatcherism.
> 2 How have Conservatives developed their ideas about social issues since the 1980s?
> 3 Why did the coronavirus pandemic present a challenge to Conservative economic ideas?
>
> **Answers on p. 126**

Labour

REVISED

Table 8.2 outlines the origins, ideas and development of the Labour Party.

Table 8.2 The Labour Party

Origins	• The Labour Representation Committee was formed in 1900 and became the Labour Party in 1906. • It included trade unions and left-wing political groups. • The aim was to represent the working class in parliament. • Labour rejected **revolutionary socialism**, focusing instead on social democracy. • The party's 1918 constitution committed Labour to socialism. • Labour formed its first government in 1929 but did not win a majority until 1945. • The 1945 Labour government created the NHS and the welfare state, and nationalised many industries. These reforms formed the basis of the post-war consensus.
Ideas	• Socialism is an ideology aiming for equality between people through common ownership of the means of production (public ownership of factories and industries) and redistribution of wealth from rich to poor. • Social democracy is the democratic version of socialism. Socialists win power within a democratic (usually capitalist) system, and introduce changes such as nationalisation, high taxation and a welfare state. • Clause IV is part of the 1918 constitution; it committed Labour to the 'common ownership of the means of production, distribution and exchange', meaning widespread nationalisation. • The 'Third Way' was an ideological compromise developed by New Labour. It balanced centre-right economic policy and centre-left social policy. • Corbynism (2015–20) was described by many as a return to **Old Labour**. It advocated the renationalisation of the railways and utilities, reversing austerity and increasing taxes on business to pay for the welfare state. • Divisions existed within the Labour movement over Brexit. Most MPs were Europhiles, supporting internationalism and EU protections on workers' rights. A small minority campaigned for Leave, arguing that freedom of movement of EU citizens undermined the wages and public services of UK workers. • Keir Starmer has emphasised the 'moral case for socialism', aiming to make it relevant to the 2020s and '30s by focusing on economic justice, social justice and climate justice.
Development	• Labour moved to the left after its 1979 defeat by Thatcher. It struggled electorally. • In 1994 Tony Blair became leader. He recognised the economic successes of Thatcherism and aimed to **triangulate** Labour's policies. With his ally Gordon Brown, he launched New Labour, which adopted the Third Way. • In 1995 Blair rewrote Clause IV, removing references to socialist economic policy. This reassured middle-class potential voters. • In 1997 Labour won a landslide victory. It implemented devolution, the removal of hereditary peers from the House of Lords, the passing of the Human Rights Act 1998 and the Freedom of Information Act 2000, the introduction of a national minimum wage and increased public spending. • Blair's reputation never recovered from his decision to commit Britain to the war in Iraq in 2003. • When Blair stood down in 2007, Gordon Brown served as prime minister until his defeat in the 2010 election. Brown had nurtured Labour's economic reputation as chancellor of the exchequer, but this was weakened by the impact of the 2008 global financial crisis. • New leader Ed Miliband moved the party slightly to the left and was vilified by right-wing newspapers. The party was defeated again in the 2015 election.

	+ Blairites called for a return to centrist policies but the party elected Jeremy Corbyn as leader in 2015.
+ Corbyn represented a dramatic break with New Labour: he was the most rebellious backbencher during Blair's government and was backed by the grassroots movement Momentum.
+ Corbyn was criticised by right-wing newspapers for being a radical socialist. Labour's share of the vote increased in 2017, but nose-dived in 2019, forcing Corbyn to resign as leader.
+ Keir Starmer became leader in 2020 and aimed to make Labour electable by tackling anti-Semitism within the party and improving Labour's appeal to working-class voters. His first year in office was dominated by the coronavirus pandemic, so he produced few policies but instead focused on providing a responsible opposition to the government's management of the crisis. He tried to show the public that he was analysing the government's policies on their merits, rather than their ideology.

Revolutionary socialism An ideology that aims to create a socialist society through revolution.

Old Labour The traditional policies and values of the Labour Party. These include a commitment to socialism, nationalisation, the welfare state, high taxation and the redistribution of wealth.

Triangulation Tony Blair's repositioning of Labour on the political spectrum, moving towards Thatcherism on economic policy but retaining traditional Labour social values.

Making links

Blair's enthusiasm for the EU led him to support the 2004 expansion of the EU to include ten more countries, mostly from Central and Eastern Europe. This caused a significant rise in immigration, which stored up future problems for Labour. Many working-class Labour voters were sceptical of immigration and the EU, which led to some switching their support to UKIP in 2015 and to the Conservatives in 2019.

Liberal Democrats

Table 8.3 outlines the origins, ideas and development of the Liberal Democrat Party.

Table 8.3 The Liberal Democrat Party

| Origins | + Formed from two different parties: the Liberal Party and the Social Democratic Party (SDP).
+ The Liberal Party was once one of the two main parties in UK politics but, after the First World War, it was pushed into third place by the Labour Party.
+ The SDP was formed in 1981, when four leading Labour politicians (the 'gang of four') left Labour in protest at its increasingly left-wing policies.
+ In 1981, the SDP formed an electoral pact with the Liberal Party, known as 'The Alliance'.
+ In 1988, the two parties merged to form the Liberal Democrats. |
|---|---|
| Ideas | + Liberalism is an ideology based on freedom. This includes individual freedom and free trade.
+ Social democracy is the democratic version of socialism. Socialists win power within a democratic (usually capitalist) system, and introduce changes such as nationalisation, high taxation and a welfare state.
+ Social liberalism is focused on a liberal form of social democracy. Social liberals are keen to dismantle Thatcher's economic policies and to redistribute wealth via higher taxation on the wealthy. Many were once members of the SDP and the Labour Party prior to that.
+ 'Orange Book' liberalism is so-called because of a book written by prominent liberals, *The Orange Book: Reclaiming Liberalism*. Unlike social liberals, these thinkers accepted the free market and did not significantly challenge Thatcherite economic policies.
+ Electoral reform is a top priority for Liberal Democrats. The Alliance famously won 26% of the vote in 1983 but only 23 seats in the House of Commons. The party argues for a proportional electoral system.
+ Unlike Labour and the Conservatives, the Liberal Democrats consistently supported the EU. |

Check your understanding and progress at www.hoddereducation.co.uk/myrevisionnotesdownloads

| Development | + Tony Blair considered forming a coalition with the Liberal Democrats, but his large majority in 1997 meant this was not necessary. The Liberal Democrats won 46 seats in 1997 with leader Paddy Ashdown.
+ Charles Kennedy oversaw the party's best result of 62 seats in 2005. This was partly a result of the party's opposition to the Iraq War.
+ Nick Clegg became leader in 2007. He gave the Liberal Democrats their first experience of government — a coalition with David Cameron's Conservatives after the 2010 election produced a hung parliament. The two men were ideally placed to form a coalition as both were towards the centre of the political spectrum: Clegg was towards the right of his party and Cameron was towards the left of his. Clegg became Cameron's deputy prime minister.
+ As part of the coalition agreement, the Liberal Democrats agreed to increase university tuition fees. Their signature pledge had been not to raise fees, so they were seen as having broken a promise and abandoned students, who were some of their core voters.
+ The coalition introduced economic austerity and reduced public spending, which alienated many of the Liberal Democrats' more left-wing supporters. The coalition erased the Liberal Democrats' unique identity: many voters were left wondering what the difference was between them and the Conservatives.
+ 2015 was a disastrous election for the Liberal Democrats: their numbers were cut to just eight MPs. Nick Clegg resigned as leader.
+ The Liberal Democrats campaigned hard for Remain during the 2016 EU referendum but were unsuccessful. They hoped to attract angry Remainers in the 2017 election but won only 14 seats. Party leader Jo Swinson lost her seat in 2019 after promising to cancel Brexit without a second referendum if she won a majority.
+ Post-Brexit, the Liberal Democrats' challenge is to articulate new ideas that will distinguish them from other parties. Ed Davey was elected leader in 2021 and said that the economy was his top priority, including green jobs and a Universal Basic Income. |
|---|---|

Now test yourself

TESTED

4 What was the name of the ideology adopted by New Labour?
5 Give three features of Corbynism.
6 What issue did the Liberal Democrats use as the focus of their 2017 and 2019 election campaigns?

Answers on p. 126

Exam tip

Remember that the Liberal Democrats stopped being the third largest party in the House of Commons in 2015, when they were overtaken by the SNP.

Current policies

The three main parties

REVISED

The 2019 policies of the three main parties in the UK are given in Table 8.4.

Table 8.4 2019 policies of the main political parties

2019 election manifesto	Conservatives	Labour	Liberal Democrats
Economy	Negotiate new free-trade agreements with other countries Support small businesses	Nationalise railways, buses, water, the big six energy companies, Royal Mail, the National Grid and part of BT Free broadband for every home and business	Support small businesses, catering, leisure and the arts
Health	50,000 new nurses, more GP appointments, 40 new hospitals, free hospital parking, increased charges for non-UK residents to use the NHS	4.3% yearly increase in spending, investment in mental health, free dental check-ups	Add 1p on income tax to fund an extra £7 billion investment a year, plus £10 billion additional capital spending Prioritise mental health

2019 election manifesto	Conservatives	Labour	Liberal Democrats
Education	£30,000 starting salary for teachers, more free schools set up, expansion of alternate provision and special educational needs places	Sure Start early years education for all children, scrap university tuition fees and reintroduce maintenance grants, remove charitable status for private schools	Free childcare from nine months for working parents, increase school funding, 20,000 new teachers
Tax	No increase to income tax, VAT or national insurance Clamp down on tax avoidance and evasion	Increase tax on highest earners Increase corporation tax and inheritance tax Introduce a tax on second homes	Increase corporation tax slightly Simplify tax system and replace business rates system
Defence	Exceed **NATO** requirement for defence spending and increase defence spending each year Set up Space Command	Increase spending on UN peacekeeping Meet NATO requirement for defence spending Support renewal of **Trident nuclear deterrent**	Meet NATO requirement for defence spending Work towards multilateral nuclear disarmament, but keep Britain's nuclear deterrent in the meantime
The environment	Carbon neutral by 2050	Carbon neutral by 2030s	Carbon neutral by 2045
Brexit	Get Brexit Done — leave the EU and return Britain's sovereignty over its laws	Renegotiate a better Brexit deal with the EU, then put it to the people in a second EU referendum	Reverse Brexit, without a second referendum

North Atlantic Treaty Organization (NATO) An international organisation of 30 Western nations including the UK, the USA, Germany, France and Turkey. Members agree to collectively protect each other's security: an aggressive attack on one NATO member is considered an act upon all. All members are committed to spend 2% of their gross domestic product (GDP) on defence.

Trident nuclear deterrent Britain's continuous at-sea nuclear deterrent, which has been in operation since 1969. The UK has four nuclear submarines, one of which is always at sea. Even if all of Britain's land-based defences were destroyed, the Trident nuclear missiles could still be fired from sea.

Exam tip

Do not be tempted to argue that the main political parties have moved closer together on the political spectrum. Although this was perhaps true for Blair's Labour Party and Cameron's Conservative Party, in recent years it has not been. Labour moved sharply to the left under Corbyn, and Boris Johnson moved the Conservatives to the right.

Political parties are always developing new policies, some of which may have been announced after this book was written. It is worth checking online to see what the most recent policies are so that you can show the examiner you are up to date.

Revision activity

Using Table 8.4, find examples of policies that link to the following ideologies:
+ one-nation conservatism
+ Thatcherism
+ socialism
+ social liberalism.

Check your understanding and progress at www.hoddereducation.co.uk/myrevisionnotesdownloads

Party structures and functions

Participation

REVISED

Figure 8.1 gives an overview of participation within a political party.

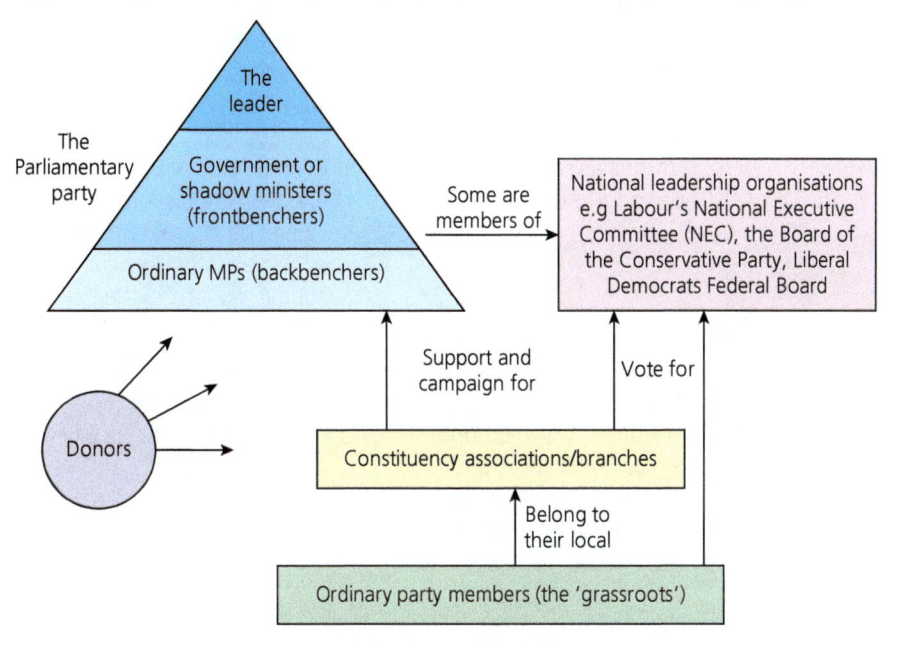

Figure 8.1 Who participates within a political party?

Functions

REVISED

- Representation: parties represent the ideology and views of their members.
- Participation: parties provide opportunities for people to participate in politics.
- Recruitment: parties recruit and select candidates for elections.
- Policy: parties develop policies and offer these to the electorate in their manifestos.
- Government: parties provide voters with a clear choice of different governments. Once elected, the party helps to organise and discipline MPs to support the government's political agenda.

> **Political agenda** The political issues that are prioritised by political parties, the media or in general public debate.

Structure and membership

REVISED

The structure and membership of the three main parties in the UK are given in Table 8.5.

Table 8.5 Structure and membership of the main political parties

	Conservatives	Labour	Liberal Democrats
Local and national structure	<ul><li>Each constituency has a Conservative Association; these help run election campaigns.</li><li>There is a Welsh Conservative Party and a Scottish Conservative Party within the UK Conservative Party.</li><li>The National Conservative Convention makes decisions for the voluntary party. Constituency association chairs attend, as do regional officers and representatives from the party's youth and women's organisations.</li></ul>	<ul><li>Each constituency has a Constituency Labour Party (CLP). Smaller local branches choose the local council candidates.</li><li>There is a Welsh Labour Party and a Scottish Labour Party within the UK Labour Party.</li><li>The National Executive Committee (NEC) is the governing body of the Labour Party.</li></ul>	<ul><li>Unlike the two main parties, the Liberal Democrats use a federal structure.</li><li>Members belong to a local party, a regional party and the national party of England, Wales or Scotland.</li><li>The Federal Board is the governing body of the Liberal Democrats, which brings together the national parties.</li></ul>

	Conservatives	Labour	Liberal Democrats
	+ The 1922 Committee is made up of backbench Conservative MPs. + Conservative Campaign Headquarters (CCHQ) is the headquarters of the party, based in London. + The Board of the Conservative Party is the governing body of the party.	+ The Parliamentary Labour Party (PLP) consists of Labour MPs. + 14 trade unions are affiliated to Labour: these are co-ordinated by the Trade Union and Labour Party Liaison Organisation. + Many socialist societies and groups are affiliated to the Labour Party.	+ There is a parliamentary party of the House of Commons made up of Liberal Democrat MPs. + Members can also join Specified Associated Organisations (SAOs): groups with a particular identity or focus, such as Ethnic Minority Liberal Democrats and the Association of Liberal Democrat Engineers and Scientists. They can submit motions to the party conference.
Membership figures	+ 200,000 (March 2021).	+ 552,000 peak in June 2017 made Labour the biggest political party in Europe — Corbyn's leadership increased membership numbers dramatically. + Still 496,000 members in 2020.	+ 115,000 (August 2019). + Significant increase in membership numbers since 44,700 in 2014.

Making links

Membership figures link to participation and democracy. The general trend of falling membership figures over the past decades might imply that participation is falling, with negative implications for democracy. However, people may be participating in new ways, such as by joining pressure groups. The recent membership growth of many UK parties suggests either that the electorate is becoming more engaged or that these parties have become more effective at attracting new members.

Appointing party leaders

REVISED

The processes for appointing party leaders are given in Table 8.6. All three parties have two rounds: one for the parliamentary party and one for all members using OMOV.

OMOV One member, one vote.

Table 8.6 Choosing and removing party leaders

Conservatives	Labour	Liberal Democrats
+ MPs vote on leadership candidates. Candidates are eliminated in voting rounds until only two remain. Their top two choices are presented to the rest of the party. + All party members vote on the remaining two candidates. It is an OMOV system, so every vote counts equally.	+ The Parliamentary Labour Party (PLP) makes nominations first: candidates need to be nominated by at least 20% of the PLP to proceed to the next round. + Candidates also need the support of 5% of local parties or 5% of trade union affiliate members. + All members then vote on candidates, using OMOV and the Alternative Vote system.	+ A candidate must be an MP, have the support of at least 10% of Liberal Democrat MPs and backing from at least 20 local parties, with support from at least 200 members. + All members vote using OMOV and the Alternative Vote system.

+ Labour's use of 'registered supporters' was controversial. In 2015 supporters who paid £3 were allowed to vote in the leadership election: more than 100,000 signed up. Some 84% supported Jeremy Corbyn, giving him a significant advantage. In 2016 the fee changed to £25, to prevent leadership elections from being hijacked by people not fully committed to

the party. Regardless of the fee hike, 180,000 people signed up as registered supporters to vote. In 2021, Keir Starmer changed the rules so that registered supporters could no longer vote in leadership elections.
+ The Conservative Party gives more power to MPs than Labour or the Liberal Democrats, as only the top two candidates progress to the second round. The eventual winner is therefore likely to have the backing of a significant number of MPs.
+ In contrast, Labour members elected Jeremy Corbyn in 2015 despite his nomination by only 15.5% of MPs. At that time, candidates only required the support of 10% of the Parliamentary Labour Party; this was increased to 20% in Starmer's 2021 rule change.

Making links

All three parties have two rounds of voting for their leader, one for the parliamentary party, and one for all members using OMOV. This was not always the case—until 1998 the Conservative leader was chosen by MPs alone. Until 2014 Labour Party members had just one-third of the votes, with trade unions and MPs holding the other two-thirds. The adoption of OMOV has made both parties more democratic internally and given members an important form of political participation.

Choosing parliamentary candidates

REVISED

All three parties use a similar procedure to choose parliamentary candidates:
1 Potential candidates are approved by the central organisation of the party.
2 The local party selects candidates from the central party list.
3 Constituency members vote to select the parliamentary candidate.

The three parties have traditionally struggled to select a broad range of candidates, which affects the composition of the House of Commons. They have tried various methods to change this. Labour introduced all-women shortlists in 1993, resulting in 101 female Labour MPs being elected in 1997 (in 1992 there were just 60 female MPs in total, 37 of whom were Labour). In September 2017 the party announced plans to use all-women shortlists for almost 50 of its top target seats.

All-women shortlists
Lists of solely female candidates for a parliamentary constituency.

The Conservatives have tried priority lists, public hustings and open primaries.
+ Priority lists are centrally prepared lists of priority (A-list) candidates, e.g. women and those from ethnic minorities. Priority candidates are offered to the local party when it draws up its shortlist for parliamentary candidates.
+ Public hustings are events where parliamentary candidates answer questions on their policies in front of the public, as well as party members.
+ Open primaries are elections in which any registered voter can choose to vote, not just party members. Open primaries are not used often, but can generate publicity for the party.

Revision activity

Explain the advantages and disadvantages of each of the following:
+ all-women shortlists
+ public hustings
+ open primaries
+ priority lists.

Revision activities

1 Give each party a score out of five for how much power it gives:
   + the grassroots
   + the leader.
2 Which party has the most internal democracy?

Exam tip

Questions on party structures and functions are likely to focus on internal democracy (the degree to which ordinary members are involved in decision making within an organisation), so make sure you learn the different ways that members can participate in decision making in each party.

My Revision Notes AQA A-level UK Politics Second Edition

Establishing party policy

REVISED

The methods for establishing party policy are given in Table 8.7.

Table 8.7 Establishing party policy

Conservatives	Labour	Liberal Democrats
+ Top-down process: the leader's team effectively decides what goes in the manifesto. + Delegates at the party conference do not vote on policy.	+ The National Policy Forum (representatives from across the party) agrees on the direction of policy and arranges policy commissions. + Policies are then voted on at the party conference. + The leader can use personal authority to win support for their policies at conference. + The leader's team then writes the manifesto, which must be agreed by the party's National Executive Committee, shadow cabinet ministers, and senior trade union representatives.	+ The Federal Policy Committee (a mix of parliamentarians and other party members) develops policies to be put to the party conference (held twice a year). + Any member can also make a policy proposal to the party conference. + The conference votes on all policies and all members can vote.

Now test yourself

TESTED

7 Which party uses a federal structure?
8 Which party has regularly used all-women shortlists to select parliamentary candidates?
9 Which party does not allow its members to vote on policy at the party conference?

Answers on p. 126

Party funding

Sources and types

REVISED

Party funding is the income received by political parties. It comes from a variety of sources, including membership fees, donations and state funding, as shown in Table 8.8.

Table 8.8 Sources of party funding

Source	Description
Membership fees	Income from these has reduced as membership numbers have fallen since the 1980s.
Small donations from individual members	The fall in membership numbers has also resulted in fewer small donations.
Large donations from wealthy donors	These are a significant source of income, particularly for the Conservative Party. Tony Blair's Labour government was criticised for accepting a £1 million donation from Formula 1 tycoon Bernie Ecclestone in 1997 and then giving Formula 1 an exemption from the ban on tobacco advertising at sporting events. Members of the elite 'Leader's Group' of Conservative donors gave more than £130 million to the party from 2010 to 2019. They received private access to the prime minister and other ministers, and almost 20% were given honours. The Conservatives receive far more individual donations than any other party: in the 2019 election, they received more than £13 million from individuals and almost £6 million from companies.
Trade unions	Labour has always received essential support from trade unions. Unions provided 93% of its donations in the 2019 general election, just over £5 million. Unions can also use their financial clout to put pressure on Labour—when Keir Starmer became leader, the largest trade union, Unite, cut funding by 10% after its general secretary, a Corbyn ally, expressed concerns about the new direction of Labour.
State funding	Designed to counter the financial advantage enjoyed by the party of government or parties with large funds.

Check your understanding and progress at www.hoddereducation.co.uk/myrevisionnotesdownloads

Different types of state funding are described in Table 8.9.

Table 8.9 Types of state funding

Type	Description
Short money	State funds paid to opposition parties in the House of Commons to cover administrative costs and to enable effective scrutiny of the government.
Cranborne money	State funds paid to opposition parties in the House of Lords to cover administrative costs and to enable effective scrutiny of the government.
Policy Development Grants (PDGs)	Any party with two or more sitting MPs is allocated a share of a £2 million annual fund to help to develop policies.
Support for election campaigns	Royal Mail will send one free campaign mailing to every elector in the UK, and parties receive free airtime for televised election broadcasts.

> **Exam tip**
>
> Remember that small parties do not receive the same amount of state funding as larger parties. Instead, they are allocated funds according to how many seats they have in parliament and how many votes they won in the last election.

> **Revision activity**
>
> List the advantages and disadvantages of each type of party funding. Remember to consider possible impacts on the party and on UK democracy in general.

Reforms

Party funding has seen several recent reforms, as shown in Table 8.10.

Table 8.10 Reforms to party funding

Reform	Description
Political Parties, Elections and Referendums Act (PPERA) 2000	+ Spending limit on party spending in general election campaigns (£30,000 per constituency) + Donations over £7500 must be declared to the Electoral Commission
Political Parties and Elections Act (PPEA) 2009	+ Allowed the Electoral Commission to investigate cases and impose fines + Increased the requirements for establishing the source of political donations

> **Making links**
>
> The influence of wealthy donors is a challenge to pluralism within our democracy. Labour was originally founded to represent working people, and union funding allowed it to avoid needing the support of the wealthy elite. As union membership numbers have fallen, unions themselves represent a smaller proportion of the population.

The media

Relations with the media

+ Newspapers may affect how party leaders are perceived. In 2019, *The Sun* described Jeremy Corbyn (Labour leader 2015–20) as 'the most dangerous man ever to stand for high office in Britain'.
+ Some party leaders have worked to develop good relationships with media bosses. Tony Blair convinced media mogul Rupert Murdoch to switch *The Sun* newspaper's support to Labour, which one study suggested won Labour an extra half a million votes. Keen to ensure their support, David Cameron met with Murdoch and his associates 26 times during his first 15 months as prime minister.
+ The *Daily Mail* and *The Telegraph* are consistent Conservative supporters, whereas *The Mirror* always favours Labour and the *Guardian* generally does.
+ Other newspapers change their endorsement with each election.
+ The BBC is a public service broadcaster, so must remain politically neutral. However, it is regularly criticised by both main parties for biased reporting.
+ Social media is increasingly important, and allows parties to target voters by age, gender and other attributes. Labour spent £1.4 million on social media in the 2019 general election, the Conservatives £900,000.

Factors affecting electoral outcomes

What factors affect electoral outcomes?

REVISED

Table 8.11 gives some of the issues that affect electoral outcomes.

Table 8.11 Factors affecting electoral outcomes

Factor	Description
Party leader	+ Media coverage is very focused on the characteristics of the party leader. + Leaders who struggle to connect with voters (e.g. Gordon Brown and Theresa May) or to impress voters (e.g. Ed Miliband) are likely to have disappointing electoral results.
Funding	+ A clear advantage to the Conservatives (wealthy donors). + Labour remains heavily dependent on trade union funding. + Parties with a chance of being in government have a big advantage as donors think they are worth giving to.
Policies	+ Appealing and well-thought-out policies (e.g. New Labour in 1997) have much greater electoral appeal than poorly crafted policies (e.g. Theresa May's 2017 plans for people to pay for home care if they had assets of more than £100,000; it was swiftly labelled the 'dementia tax' and had to be scrapped).
Record	+ Governments are judged on their record, e.g. in 1997 John Major's Conservative government was punished for sleaze; in 2015 the Liberal Democrats were punished for their role in the coalition.
The media	+ Support from key newspapers such as *The Sun* may be helpful. + Social media is increasingly important.
Election campaigns	+ A well-crafted election campaign can help to secure a landslide (e.g. New Labour in 1997) or a big win (Get Brexit Done, Conservatives 2019). + A poorly crafted campaign can cause the popularity of a party and its leader to nosedive (e.g. Theresa May in 2017).
Overton window	+ The 'window' of public opinion in terms of ideas: any ideas outside the window will not be tolerated by the public. + Parties who keep their policies within the Overton window are much more likely to be elected. + Other factors can be more important: Labour's socialist policies were popular in 2019—a YouGov poll found 60% of the public supported the increased tax on high earners and 56% agreed with nationalising the railways—but 70% of people had a negative opinion of Jeremy Corbyn.
Electoral system and strategy	+ FPTP favours parties with concentrated geographical support, e.g. the SNP. + Electoral pacts can help parties win. The Brexit Party's decision not to contest Conservative-held seats in 2019 helped the Conservatives win a large majority, while Labour was criticised for failing to make a Remain Alliance electoral pact with other parties.

> **Now test yourself** TESTED
>
> 10 What are the most important sources of party funding for the Conservatives and Labour?
> 11 What is the name for the public funds given to opposition parties in the House of Commons?
> 12 Who owns *The Sun* newspaper and why is he politically important?
>
> Answers on p. 126

> **Exam tip**
>
> Do not assume that the media necessarily influence voters. Newspapers certainly try to shape public opinion, but it is unclear how far they influence their readers or whether they simply reflect their readers' views.

Minor parties

Policies of minor parties

REVISED

Minor parties are those other than the main national parties and include so-called 'single-issue' parties, such as UKIP and the Green Party, and nationalist parties such as the SNP and Plaid Cymru. Minor parties can be very important — the SNP is in government in Scotland and is the third largest party in the House of Commons. Table 8.12 outlines the policies of the main minor parties and their impact on political debates and the political agenda.

Table 8.12 Minor parties

Party	Policies	Impact on political debates and the political agenda
Scottish National Party (SNP)	Independence for Scotland Increase public spending, especially on health End austerity Scrap the Trident nuclear deterrent and use the savings for public services	+ Won a majority in the 2011 Scottish Parliament elections, allowing the SNP to pressure the UK government for a referendum. + Scotland voted to remain in the UK in 2014, so the SNP did not achieve its core objective. + However, SNP membership increased, resulting in a landslide victory in Scotland in the 2015 general election (56 of 59 seats). + The SNP lost seats in 2017 (winning 35 seats) but won another landslide in 2019, with 48 seats. + It is the third-largest party in the UK parliament, and has been in government in Scotland since 2007. + Responsible for managing the coronavirus pandemic in Scotland. + First Minister Nicola Sturgeon has called for a second independence referendum as Scotland voted to remain in the EU, but was taken out by the UK government.
UK Independence Party (UKIP)	Keep the UK totally separate from the EU Anti-immigration Free speech, free markets	+ Founded in 1993, UKIP gradually built support. + Won the 2014 European Parliament elections, pushing the Conservatives into third place. + Fears that many Conservative voters would switch to UKIP in the 2015 general election prompted David Cameron to pledge an EU referendum if he won a majority. + UKIP's general election results are limited by FPTP: it won 3.9 million votes in 2015 but just one seat in the House of Commons. + Achieved its core objective when Britain voted to leave the EU in 2016. + Struggled to define a clear purpose for itself post-Brexit and has lacked a convincing leader since the resignation of Nigel Farage in 2016. + UKIP won fewer than 29,000 votes in the 2019 election and no seats in parliament.
Reform UK (known as the Brexit Party from 2018 to 2020)	Low-tax economy Reform public sector, institutions and electoral system Opposition to coronavirus restrictions and lockdowns	+ Founded as the Brexit Party by former UKIP leader Nigel Farage in 2018, to push for a clean break with the EU. + Won the 2019 European Parliament elections, with 31% of the vote. Its success may have influenced Conservative Party members to choose pro-leave Boris Johnson as their leader a few weeks later. + Chose not to contest Conservative-held seats in the 2019 election to avoid splitting the leave vote. This tactic may have doubled Johnson's majority. The Brexit Party did not win any seats. + Renamed as Reform UK in 2020 to create a post-Brexit identity for itself, initially focused on opposing coronavirus restrictions.
Plaid Cymru	Independence for Wales Increased investment in Wales	+ Provides a clear voice for Wales and consistently argues in favour of increased public spending. + Struggles for media attention because of its size: it won just four seats in the 2019 general election.

Party	Policies	Impact on political debates and the political agenda
Democratic Unionist Party (DUP)	Northern Ireland to remain fully part of the UK, with no border checks in the Irish Sea Socially conservative: opposes same-sex marriage and abortion	+ Largest unionist party in Northern Ireland. + In government in Northern Ireland with Sinn Féin, as part of the power-sharing agreement introduced by the Good Friday Agreement (1998). + Won eight seats in the UK Parliament in 2019. + Supported the Conservative minority government from 2017 to 2019 in a confidence and supply deal (meaning they agreed to support the government in any vote of no confidence, or a budget vote, and on certain pieces of legislation). This gave the DUP considerable influence in the UK government. + Campaigned for Brexit in 2016. + Opposed Boris Johnson's EU withdrawal deal as it meant that Northern Ireland would be treated differently to the rest of the UK, in order to avoid a hard border with Ireland.
Sinn Féin	Special status for Northern Ireland's relationship with the EU, to ensure no hard border in Ireland Referendum to unite Northern Ireland with the Republic of Ireland	+ Largest nationalist party in Northern Ireland. + In government in Northern Ireland with its rival, the DUP. + Sinn Féin MPs do not take up their seats in the UK parliament, because they believe Northern Ireland should not be part of the UK. The party was criticised for this during May's minority government, when their seven votes might have helped Remainers in crucial votes on the Brexit deal.
Green Party	Environmental protections and a green economy Investment in public services	+ Provides an environmental perspective on all policy areas. + Limited direct influence over policy because of its size: it only won one seat in the 2019 general election. + Encourages other progressive parties to develop environmental policies to compete for green votes. Keeps green issues on the political agenda. + Helped the Liberal Democrats to win two marginal seats in 2017 by encouraging Green supporters to vote Liberal Democrat to keep the Conservatives out. + United with the Liberal Democrats and Plaid Cymru in an electoral pact in 2019, but did not win more seats.

> **Exam tip**
>
> Remember that minor parties can still have a significant impact on the political agenda, even if they have very limited representation in parliament. UKIP provides the best example of this: despite only ever winning one seat in the UK parliament (in 2015), it was able to pressure the Conservatives into calling a referendum on EU membership. It transformed the political agenda, and the UK's future.

> **Making links**
>
> Electoral systems were key to UKIP's rise and fall. The regional list proportional representation system allowed it to win the European Parliament elections in 2014, but FPTP stopped it from making an impact in the UK Parliament.
>
> The FPTP system makes it very difficult for new parties to break into UK politics, as demonstrated by the failure of the Independent Group for Change. This centrist party was founded by pro-remain MPs from Labour and the Tories in 2019. Some ten months later, all its MPs lost their seats in the 2019 election, and the party was dissolved.

Party systems

Development towards a multi-party system

REVISED

Table 8.13 summarises the party systems in the UK.

> **Party system** The number of significant political parties operating in a country. Party systems include one-party (e.g. China), dominant-party (e.g. South Africa), two-party (e.g. USA) and multi-party (e.g. many European countries using proportional representation).

Table 8.13 What kind of party system does the UK have?

Party system	Definition	UK evidence in favour
Two-party system	Two significant political parties compete for power in a duopoly A typical product of FPTP electoral systems Tends to result in single-party majority governments	+ Either the Conservatives or Labour have been in government since 1922. There have been several periods of coalition, but the two major parties have provided every prime minister. + Since the 1930s, only the Conservatives and Labour have had a realistic chance of winning a general election and forming or leading the UK government. Together they won 87% of seats in 2019. + FPTP has prevented smaller parties from winning a proportional number of seats to their votes. + Coalition and minority governments have been rare in UK politics traditionally. + The 2017 election was described as a return to two-party politics as, together, Labour and the Conservatives won over 80% of votes for the first time since the 1980s. Their vote share was nearly as high in 2019, at almost 76%.
Multi-party system	Multiple significant political parties compete for power A typical product of proportional voting systems Tends to result in coalitions or minority governments	+ In recent years smaller parties have played a key role in government: the Liberal Democrats held important positions in the 2010–15 coalition government; the 2017–19 Conservative minority government was dependent on the DUP. + Smaller parties have had a significant impact on UK politics: the SNP's dominance in Scottish general elections from 2015 made it more difficult for the Conservatives or Labour to win a majority, and UKIP's rise prompted the Conservative government to hold the 2016 EU referendum. + Multiple parties hold power across the UK and devolved nations: as of January 2022, the UK, Scotland, Wales and Northern Ireland were all headed by governments from different political parties.

> **Making links**
> Proponents of electoral reform argue that FPTP is undemocratic because it prevents the UK party system from reflecting the true wishes of the British electorate. In the last proportional election—the 2019 European Parliament elections—the Conservatives came fifth, not only finishing behind the Brexit Party (who won), but also the Liberal Democrats, Labour and the Green Party. Adopting a proportional system in UK general elections would encourage coalitions and might allow a more accurate representation of the people's views within government.

> **Making links**
> Different types of electoral systems produce different party systems. You can learn more about the impact of electoral systems on the party system in Chapter 7.

> ### Now test yourself
>
> TESTED
>
> 13 Which party made a confidence and supply deal with the Conservatives in 2017?
> 14 Which minor party has achieved its main aim?
> 15 Which type of electoral system tends to produce a multi-party system?
> 16 When did the UK last have a coalition government?
>
> **Answers on p. 126**

Exam tip

If you are asked which type of party system the UK has, refer to the definition of a party system: the number of significant political parties operating in a country. If 'significant' means 'leading the UK government', then the UK has a two-party system. If a broader definition is used, such as 'wielding considerable political power', then the UK could certainly be considered to be a multi-party system, particularly when the devolved nations are considered.

Summary

You should now have an understanding of:
- the origins, ideas and development of the Conservative, Labour and Liberal Democrat parties
- the party structures and functions of the Conservative, Labour and Liberal Democrat parties
- how party funding works and the rules that regulate it
- factors affecting electoral outcomes, including the relationship between parties and the media
- the policies of minor parties and their impact on political debates and the political agenda
- party systems and the development towards a multi-party system in the UK and its impact on government and policy.

Exam practice

1 Explain and analyse three features of party funding. [9]
2 'Minor parties have had little impact on the political agenda.' Analyse and evaluate this statement. [25]
3 'Labour is a socialist party.' Analyse and evaluate this statement. [25]

Answers available online

9 Pressure groups

Key points

REVISED

- A pressure group is an organisation that aims to influence political decision making. For example, the NSPCC (National Society for the Prevention of Cruelty to Children) campaigns to encourage the government and parliament to introduce policies and laws to protect children.
- Pressure groups differ from political parties because they seek only to influence those in power, whereas a political party aims to win political power for itself.
- Pressure groups can be very small, such as a local conservation group with only a handful of members, while other pressure groups can have huge memberships. Unite is the largest trade union in the UK, with 1.4 million members. Many pressure groups are part of broader social movements.

> **Social movements** Long-term campaigns for the improvement of an aspect of society. Examples include the labour, women's, environmental and LGBTQ+ rights movements, and more recent movements such as #FridaysForFuture and Black Lives Matter. Social movements are less structured and organised than pressure groups and may include pressure groups within them. For example, the environmental movement includes pressure groups such as Greenpeace and Friends of the Earth.

Typologies

Insider and outsider groups

REVISED

Insider groups are those that are consulted by the government and therefore have insider status. Insider groups need to be law abiding with a good public image to retain the trust of the government. For example, the British Medical Association (BMA) is consulted as a matter of course on health-related matters.

Outsider groups are those that are not consulted by the government and instead try to influence political decision making from the outside. Some outsider groups work towards insider status, whereas others are ideologically opposed to the government and happy to remain outsiders. For example, Stop Huntingdon Animal Cruelty (SHAC) used extreme tactics that were incompatible with insider status.

Case study

Insider group: the British Medical Association (BMA)

Main aims	+ Acts as the doctors' trade union, to improve pay and conditions. + Lobbies the government for improvements to healthcare and public health, e.g. a minimum unit price for alcohol sales, a sugar tax on drinks.
Membership	+ Almost 160,000 doctors and medical students.
Methods	+ The BMA briefs MPs on health policy, meets with ministers and responds to consultations. + Organised the first full strike by junior doctors (including emergency care) in April 2016, over changes to the junior doctors' contract.

Successes	+ Plays a leading role in every debate about public health and healthcare. + One of the most respected insider groups: influences the government as it develops policies. + During the coronavirus pandemic the BMA led calls for adequate PPE for NHS workers, and secured a national inquiry into the impact of Covid-19 on healthcare staff from ethnic minorities. It released numerous public statements on different aspects of the pandemic, generating media attention and holding the government to account by emphasising the importance of following scientific advice. In June 2021, the government pushed back the lifting of coronavirus restrictions by four weeks after the BMA advised delay. + The government has introduced many policies championed by the BMA, including an opt-out system for organ donation (enacted in 2020), a sugar tax on fizzy drinks (2018), a smoking ban in enclosed public places (2007) and compulsory seatbelts for all occupants of cars (1991).
Failures	+ The BMA cancelled plans for a second junior doctors' strike in September 2016 after junior doctors complained that hospitals had not been given long enough to prepare. + The government did not give in to junior doctors: the new contract was imposed on them in October 2016. + Although the BMA is an effective *promotional group* (see p. 99), its inability to avoid the new contract suggests that it is less effective as an *interest group*. It was also unable to prevent doctors from taking a real-terms pay cut in 2021, despite their immense contribution to the pandemic response.

Case study

Outsider group: Extinction Rebellion

Main aims	+ Make government tell the truth by declaring a climate emergency. + Force government to act now, stopping further biodiversity loss and going carbon neutral by 2025. + Convince government to create a Citizens' Assembly to make decisions on how to deal with the climate emergency.
Membership	+ No formal hierarchy or formal membership—it has a decentralised structure of affiliated small activist groups. Affiliated groups plan their own actions within XR's broad aims. + Set up in 2018, by 2020 it had around 485 groups in more than 70 countries, with about 130 groups in the UK.
Methods	+ Peaceful direct action and civil disobedience. + Mass protests, e.g. blocking roads or buildings, gluing themselves to buildings and train carriages, spraying the Treasury building with fake blood. + Mass arrests, which are intended to fill police cells—1828 protesters were arrested in October 2019.
Successes	+ The environment sits higher on the political agenda than it has ever done: all major UK political parties have committed to making the UK carbon neutral (though not as quickly as XR would like—the government is aiming for 2050). + The environment matters to voters, especially the young: 26% of voters, and 45% of 18- to 24-year-olds, put it in their top three issues before the 2019 election. + Select committees in the UK Parliament set up the 100-member Citizens' Assembly UK, which met during 2020 and then wrote a report. XR said that the assembly did not meet its requirements, however, as its recommendations could be ignored by the government, and it focused on getting carbon neutral by 2050, which XR believes is far too late. + Scotland also set up a Climate Assembly but XR refused to attend, claiming it was controlled by civil servants and 'not a good enough response to the climate emergency'.
Failures	+ Criticism of some of its actions for being unhelpful 'stunts', particularly a 2019 demonstration that disrupted the London public transport network, delaying around half a million commuters. + The pace of government and intergovernmental action has not matched that demanded by XR: there may be a sense of urgency, but not emergency. + Divisions and splits have hampered the group, and its lack of hierarchy means that local groups may carry out unsuitable actions. + XR lost momentum during the first coronavirus lockdown when it was forced to 'hibernate'. Black Lives Matter subsequently dominated the political agenda in the summer of 2020, making it harder for XR to attract media attention.

Check your understanding and progress at www.hoddereducation.co.uk/myrevisionnotesdownloads

Limitations of this classification

+ Some groups are only consulted occasionally and have little real influence over government. These are known as peripheral insiders.
+ Insider groups can become outsider groups, and vice versa. Some vary depending on which party is in government. For example, trade unions have traditionally been consulted more by Labour governments.
+ Even if a group is consulted by government regularly, it may have limited influence if they fundamentally disagree. For example, the BMA failed to convince the government to improve the junior doctors' new contract.
+ On the other hand, an outsider group might be asked to give evidence to a select committee, as Extinction Rebellion was in 2019. This insider activity does not change its overall outsider status.

Promotional and interest groups

REVISED

+ Promotional groups are those that promote a specific cause, such as the housing and homelessness charity Shelter.
+ They are generally inclusive (members need not have a personal connection to their cause in order to join, unlike interest groups) and altruistic (members join to improve the greater good of society, not for their own benefit).
+ They may build mass memberships to demonstrate public support for their cause.
+ Interest groups are those that exist to defend the interests of a particular group or section of society.
+ All trade unions are interest groups as they protect the interests of their members, such as the National Education Union (NEU), the UK's largest teaching union.

Limitations of this classification

Some pressure groups do not fit neatly into the promotional and interest group classification. For example, the BMA is a promotional group as it campaigns for better public health, but *also* an interest group as it campaigns for better pay and conditions for its members.

Exam tip

Do not get confused by the two main classifications of pressure groups and assume that, as there are four different types, a pressure group can belong to only one of the four types. In reality, the two classifications exist alongside each other, so pressure groups are simultaneously either an insider or an outsider group *and* either a promotional or an interest group. For example, the mental health charity Mind is a promotional group that has insider status.

Revision activity

Make a set of flashcards to include different types of pressure groups (with at least one example for each) and the case studies given here.

Now test yourself

TESTED

1. What is the difference between a pressure group and a political party?
2. What is the opposite of an insider group?
3. What is the opposite of an interest group?
4. Give two examples of policy areas where the BMA has been successful.
5. Give an example of a BMA campaign that was unsuccessful.
6. Why are Extinction Rebellion's methods both a potential strength and a weakness?

Answers on p. 126–7

Methods used

Working within the system

REVISED

Some pressure groups work within the governmental system by targeting different access points. Table 9.1 summarises the methods used to campaign within the governmental system.

> **Access points** Points at which pressure groups can seek to influence decision makers. These include local government, devolved governments and legislatures, the UK government, parliament and the judiciary.

> **Making links**
>
> Before Brexit, the EU was also an important access point. Many pressure groups lobbied the European Commission and EU Parliament. You can learn more about the EU in Chapter 10.

Table 9.1 Working within the governmental system

Method	Description
Influencing government	+ Insider groups try to directly influence ministers and civil servants through contributions to consultations or face-to-face meetings.
Influencing parliament	+ Pressure groups lobby MPs to try to influence their votes on government bills. + They try to convince MPs to introduce a private members' bill for their cause. + They can be asked to appear before a backbench committee. Committee reports are considered seriously by the government and often reported by the media. + They may lobby the House of Lords to amend or improve government legislation, to initiate their own legislation or to put an issue on the political agenda by debating it.
Influencing political parties	+ Unions have been part of the Labour Party since its formation and make an essential financial contribution. + Some pressure groups attend party conferences to try to influence members and key figures.
Using the courts	+ Pressure groups may try to overturn government decisions with legal action using judicial review. + Publicity and changing public opinion may help the group's cause, even if the case is lost. + The Criminal Justice and Courts Act 2015 made it more difficult for charities to use judicial review, as the government claimed they used it too often to delay legislation.

> **Making links**
>
> Judicial review is an important way that individuals and pressure groups can hold the government to account for its actions. You can learn more about judicial review and the judiciary in Chapter 4.

> **Exam tip**
>
> Do not overstate the influence of trade unions on the Labour Party. Unions are important financial contributors, but not all Labour Party leaders have been heavily influenced by them. Tony Blair offered 'fairness not favours' to unions. His government faced challenges such as the 2002 firefighters' strikes, and was widely criticised by the trade union movement in general.

> **Making links**
>
> You can learn more about the Labour Party and the role of trade unions in party funding in Chapter 8.

Check your understanding and progress at www.hoddereducation.co.uk/myrevisionnotesdownloads

Working outside the system

REVISED

Other groups work outside the governmental system, usually by targeting public opinion. Table 9.2 summarises the methods used to campaign outside the governmental system.

Table 9.2 Working outside the governmental system

Method	Description
Appealing to the public	+ Pressure groups attract public support by using the media. + All pressure groups benefit from public support, but it is especially important for outsider groups. + They appeal to the public directly using social media and online campaigning. + Demonstrations and marches can bring important issues to the public's attention and show widespread support for a cause, e.g. the Black Lives Matter summer 2020 protests across the UK highlighted systemic racism.
Background campaigns	+ Long-term educational and propaganda campaigns are designed to produce significant shifts in public opinion (e.g. the environmental 'reduce, reuse and recycle' campaign or the anti-smoking campaign).
Short-term campaigns	+ These are aimed at warning the public about a specific problem and trying to solve it. + The most extreme version is the 'fire brigade campaign', a dramatic campaign designed to rally support quickly and force the government to make rapid change.
Direct action	+ This is any action taken by a pressure group beyond the usual constitutional methods of campaigning. The aim is to influence public opinion and produce a policy change by government. + Direct action includes commonly used tactics (e.g. marches, demonstrations and strikes) and more unusual headline-grabbing stunts (e.g. climbing buildings and blocking airport runways). + Some direct action is legal (e.g. trade union strikes), but some is illegal civil disobedience (e.g. environmental protesters blocking access to fracking sites). + In its most extreme form, direct action can include violence (e.g. anti-lockdown protests in London turned violent in 2020 and 2021) and harassment (e.g. Stop Huntingdon Animal Cruelty (SHAC) harassed and attacked individuals linked to the Huntingdon Life Sciences animal testing centre until it was disbanded in 2014) or even terrorism. + Unlike most direct action, which aims to win publicity and public support, violent direct action is intended to forcibly compel the government to change policy.

Now test yourself

TESTED

7 What legal method can pressure groups sometimes use to challenge the legality of government action?
8 What is the term for a long-term pressure group campaign that intends to educate the public?
9 What is the term for campaigning that may involve demonstrations, stunts or even violence?

Answers on p. 127

Exam tips

Do not assume that all direct action is the same. The term covers a range of legal and illegal activities, from striking to arson, which may be violent or non-violent.

Learn examples of the different methods used by specific pressure groups, so that you can use these in the exam.

The influence of pressure groups

Factors that affect pressure group influence

REVISED

The factors in Table 9.3 determine how much political influence a pressure group has.

Table 9.3 Factors likely to affect the political influence of pressure groups

Factor	Description
Membership	+ Large memberships often have more influence with the government. + Pressure groups with highly regarded memberships are likely to have more influence on politicians, the public and the media (e.g. the BMA is made up of doctors whose professional expertise is widely respected). + However, the government may ignore pressure groups with large memberships (e.g. striking unions) or influential memberships (e.g. the BMA doctors' strike in 2016).
Resources	+ Money funds offices, equipment, staff and advertising, helping pressure groups to influence decision makers. For example, the Confederation of British Industry (CBI) has 13 offices across the UK (and in five areas of the world), helping it to lobby government in the interests of British business. + Resources are needed to fund legal challenges to government policy. Large sums of money are needed for judicial reviews, unless the membership possesses the necessary expertise. For example, ClientEarth is an environmental law charity that has won multiple legal victories against the government's air pollution policy.
Aims	+ Limited and easily achievable aims are more likely to be met. For example, the Snowdrop Campaign was set up after the Dunblane massacre of 1996 and aimed to ban private ownership of handguns in the UK. This was straightforward to achieve and an Act of Parliament was passed in 1997.
Public support	+ Public support helps to convince politicians to support and prioritise the pressure group's cause. For example, growing public awareness of the dangers from climate change, reinforced by scientific research, encouraged all major parties to commit to making the UK carbon neutral in their 2019 election manifestos.
Methods and strategy	+ Pressure groups that target the appropriate access points for their cause will have a better chance of influencing political decision makers. + Direct action needs to be handled carefully: stunts can bring media attention and help to influence politicians, but violent and dangerous campaigning is likely to alienate decision makers and the public. + A good example of counterproductive methods is the SHAC group, which was forced to end its campaign in 2014 and 'reassess' its methods. These had been directed at people linked to animal testing and included blackmail, damage to property, sending hoax bombs and items supposedly contaminated with HIV, and falsely exposing staff as paedophiles. The result was heavy prison sentences for some of its members, and new laws to protect animal-testing services.
Celebrity endorsement	+ Endorsement can bring publicity to an issue that might otherwise be overlooked by politicians. When the pandemic forced schools to close in 2020, professional footballer Marcus Rashford became an ambassador for FareShare, a national network of food redistributors. Rashford convinced the government to perform a major policy u-turn and provide more support for children from low-income families, so they would not go hungry without free school meals.
Links with political parties	+ Trade union donations are hugely important to Labour, providing the majority of its funding for its 2019 election campaign. However, unions do not always enjoy guaranteed influence. + Political parties can approach pressure groups to gain support for a new policy. + Endorsement from a respected pressure group can boost the policy's credibility. For example, the BMA supported Labour's 2007 smoking ban.
Links with government	+ Pressure groups are generally experts in their area, whereas civil servants or ministers may not be. This expertise can be helpful to the government. + Insider status can allow pressure groups to directly influence government policy, as was the case with the BMA and the 2007 smoking ban. + Different governments will be influenced by different pressure groups. For example, Labour governments are traditionally more influenced by trade unions than Conservative governments.

Factor	Description
Relationship with the media	+ Most pressure groups aim to attract publicity from the media, particularly when carrying out direct action. They inform the media of what they are planning so that journalists can be there to document it.
	+ Media support can put pressure on politicians. For example, the media was supportive of the aims of the Snowdrop Campaign. + Media criticism of pressure groups helps the government to justify ignoring their demands. For example, most newspapers criticised the BMA's 2016 doctors' strike.
Legal victories	+ Judicial review can force the government to change policy. + The Stonehenge Alliance took the government to court over its planned £1.7 billion road and tunnel project at the World Heritage Site. In 2021, the High Court ruled the development unlawful as the government had failed to fully consider the impact of the scheme, or other options.

Exam tips

Media *attention* is not the same as media *support*. Both SHAC and the English Defence League received considerable media attention but were widely condemned by the media for their extreme tactics.

Publicity does not automatically guarantee influence. The biggest UK public protest, the 2003 march of over 1 million people against the Iraq War, did not change government policy.

You may be asked how pressure groups influence the *political agenda*. This is slightly different to how they influence the *government*. The political agenda simply means the most important political issues of the day and can be determined by the public or media, rather than the government. An issue can be high on the political agenda but ignored by the government, such as the opposition to the Iraq War in 2003.

Revision activity

1 Write the different factors that contribute to pressure group influence around the sides of a piece of paper, leaving space between them.
2 Summarise the information in Table 9.3 into no more than 25 words for each factor and add these to your diagram.
3 Make links between the different factors, adding these to your diagram and writing an explanation for each one.

Now test yourself

10 Which of the main political parties is most likely to favour trade unions?
11 How has ClientEarth successfully challenged the government?
12 Which professional footballer's intervention resulted in a change to government policy on free school meal vouchers during the pandemic?

Answers on p. 127

Other influences on government and parliament

Other influences

There are other influences on government and parliament, as shown in Table 9.4.

Table 9.4 Other influences on government and parliament

Influence	Description
Think tanks	+ Think tanks are organisations that exist purely to develop new ideas and policies. + They are funded privately by donations from individuals, groups or business. + Some have a clear position on the political spectrum. The Institute for Public Policy Research (IPPR) is a left-of-centre think tank that aims to develop progressive policies. The Institute of Economic Affairs (IEA) is right-wing and supports neo-liberal, free-market ideas. + Others seek to be independent and neutral, e.g. Chatham House, an international policy think tank, or the King's Fund, an independent think tank focused on improving health and care in England. + Think tanks are usually independent of political parties but aim to convince political parties or the government to adopt their ideas.

Influence	Description
	+ Many politicians have close links with think tanks, e.g. Iain Duncan Smith, former leader of the Conservatives, set up the Centre for Social Justice in 2004. The UK's oldest political think tank, the Fabian Society, is affiliated to the Labour Party. + Think tanks produce detailed policy, reports and research, which can be used by political parties. + They may be consulted directly by political parties or government when formulating policy. The IEA worked with Conservative Brexiteers and met with government ministers regularly during the Brexit negotiations, and pushed for a hard Brexit. + They frequently appear in the media to comment on policy debates.
Lobbyists	+ Lobbyists are political operatives who are paid to influence the government. + They are usually employed by corporations or wealthy pressure groups. Some hire independent lobbying firms, others have their own 'in-house' lobbyists. + Lobbyists arrange meetings with influential politicians and try to convince them to support the aims of their employer. + Lobbying has grown in the UK over the last two decades. In 2010, David Cameron pledged to tackle the influence of this £2 billion industry, and set up a watchdog to monitor lobbying activity. + Many former UK politicians or political advisers become lobbyists, using their contacts to gain access to current government officials. The 2021 Greensill scandal saw former Prime Minister David Cameron being investigated by the watchdog he had previously set up, for lobbying the government on behalf of financial firm Greensill Capital. Cameron was employed by Greensill as an adviser and had millions of pounds of stock options in the company. Cameron repeatedly texted Rishi Sunak, Chancellor of the Exchequer, asking for emergency funding for the company. He was cleared of wrongdoing but the Treasury Select Committee found he had acted with a 'significant lack of judgement' by using his personal connections in this way. + There have been various 'cash for access' scandals, including one in 2015 in which Jack Straw (Labour) and Sir Malcolm Rifkind (Conservative), both former foreign secretaries, were caught on camera offering to lobby for companies in return for large sums of money. Although legal, this demonstrated the access that lobbyists can have.
Corporations	+ Corporations may be invited by the government to contribute to policy discussions and to help produce legislation relevant to their business. + They lobby the government (often using professional lobbyists) for favourable conditions of business such as low taxes, fewer regulations and better infrastructure. + They may threaten to leave the UK entirely or relocate some of their business to another country if the government does not meet their demands. + Large multinational companies (e.g. Google and Amazon) can structure their business across several countries, resisting UK government attempts to make them pay more tax. + Governments are wary of alienating big businesses as they are crucial to the economy and employ many people. They also generate tax revenue. + Many owners of large corporations also make donations to political parties, particularly the Conservatives. + Most big companies actively campaigned for Remain during the 2016 EU referendum (although a minority supported Leave). They were ignored by the British public, so in this important decision their influence was limited. + Corporations lobbied the government over the details of the Brexit deal. + During the coronavirus pandemic they secured essential government support, including the furlough scheme, loans, deferred payments and business rates relief. + Many corporations fund think tanks that support their aims, e.g. British American Tobacco has made regular donations to the Institute of Economic Affairs (IEA), which opposed plain cigarette packaging.
The media	+ Governments are scrutinised by the media, and are keen to attract positive reports: communication with the media is a key priority for every government. + Government ministers often have personal links with key figures in the media, e.g. in 2012 the close friendship between Prime Minister David Cameron and Rebekah Brooks, former editor of the *News of the World* and *The Sun*, was revealed. Boris Johnson even wrote a lucrative weekly column for *The Telegraph* before he became prime minister. + Support from newspapers can help governments win elections and increase enthusiasm for their policies within parliament and across the country.

Check your understanding and progress at www.hoddereducation.co.uk/myrevisionnotesdownloads

> **Making links**
>
> Think tanks can be important in the development of political ideas. Right-wing think tanks such as the IEA are said to have inspired the development of neo-liberal Thatcherism, shifting the direction of the Conservative Party and public policy.
>
> The US lobbying industry is even bigger than the UK's. The process of ministers moving between government jobs and lobbying is known as the 'revolving door' and is also controversial in the USA.

> **Now test yourself** TESTED
>
> 13 What is the difference between a think tank and a political party?
> 14 What is a lobbyist?
> 15 Why did the EU referendum demonstrate that the influence of big business on politics has limits?
>
> **Answers on p. 127**

Pluralism

What is pluralism? REVISED

Pluralism describes a situation in which different groups, including pressure groups, compete equally for power and influence. Power is therefore spread across different groups in society. It is the opposite of elitism—the idea that powerful elites dominate society and government.

Table 9.5 assesses whether pressure groups are good for democracy.

Table 9.5 Are pressure groups good for democracy?

Yes	No
+ The pluralist interpretation is that pressure groups are an essential part of democracy as they allow different sections of society to be heard by government. + Pressure groups allow people to focus on one issue that concerns them (e.g. the environment), although that might not be their prime concern in an election. Governments must be held to account for things that do not win elections but which still matter. + Pressure groups allow people to participate in democracy at any time, rather than just during an election campaign every five years. + Many pressure groups have more members than political parties, suggesting they are more relevant to the public. + Pressure groups provide the government with information and statistics it might otherwise not discover. This is good for democracy as it makes the government better informed. + Since the passing of the 2016 Trade Union Act, unions have been prevented from striking with low internal support. They need a minimum turnout of 50% for strike ballots and a 40% threshold of support for emergency services. This ensures that strikes have a strong democratic mandate from union members.	+ The elitist interpretation is that pressure groups are undemocratic: they give a louder voice to the most powerful. Rich, educated and well-connected people are better able to form influential pressure groups than the poor and disadvantaged, and can afford to hire expensive lobbyists and lawyers. + Pressure groups often have limited internal democracy so do not truly represent their members. Decisions can be made by the leadership without consulting members. + Unlike political parties, pressure groups are unaccountable to the electorate. + Pressure groups focus on one particular issue to the exclusion of everything else. They may prevent politicians from delivering joined-up government (see p. 33). + Violent and aggressive campaigning methods (used by a small minority of pressure groups) are contrary to the rule of law and liberal democracy. + The New Right interpretation (associated with Thatcher's Conservative government) argued that trade union strikes and direct action were an attempt to undermine the democratic state. Douglas Hurd (Thatcher's foreign secretary) described pressure groups as 'serpents that strangle efficient government'.

Now test yourself

TESTED

16 Why do pluralists think that pressure groups are good for democracy?
17 Which of the main political parties has been most critical of trade unions?
18 Why could it be argued that pressure groups are more important for participation than political parties?

Answers on p. 127

Exam tip

Make sure you explain pluralism in any essay on pressure groups and democracy, as it is specifically mentioned in the specification.

Revision activity

Rank the arguments that pressure groups are good for democracy in Table 9.5 in order of how convincing they are, starting with the most convincing argument. Then do the same for the arguments against pressure groups being good for democracy.

Exam skills

Always take five minutes to plan an essay before you start writing. Think carefully about what the question is asking, and highlight the key words. You'll need to focus on those words throughout to avoid writing a 'generic' essay. Do not try to write everything you know about pressure groups, instead focus on selecting the knowledge that answers the specific question you have been asked.

When planning, you need to decide what you are going to write about, and what your overall argument will be. For example, in an essay about pressure group success, you need to evaluate what makes pressure groups successful. This means considering the different factors in Table 9.3, deciding which is the most important, and justifying your decision. If you find it difficult to decide which factor is the most important in determining pressure group influence, look for links between the different factors. If one factor influences many others, it may well be the most important.

In your essay you'll need to write a paragraph about each factor, starting with the one in the question, followed by the most important. Under timed conditions most students will only write about three or four paragraphs (excluding the introduction and the conclusion), so make sure to pick three or four really important factors to base your essay around.

Finally, think about which examples you are going to use, and how you can use them effectively. Students often make statements about pressure groups, such as 'the BMA is an insider group, which makes it successful', without giving examples of *how* the pressure group has been successful. For example: 'In 2007, the Labour government imposed a smoking ban. This is an example of how the BMA used its insider status to achieve success, as it lobbied the government for change and was consulted as part of the legislative process.' Note the use of the key word 'success', coupled with a detailed example that is analysed in relation to the question.

Summary

You should now have an understanding of:
+ different typologies of pressure groups, including insider and outsider groups, promotional groups and interest groups
+ insider and outsider group case studies: the successes and failures of the BMA and Extinction Rebellion
+ pressure group methods, including those used within the governmental system and those used outside the governmental system
+ how pressure groups influence the government
+ other influences on the government and parliament, including think tanks, lobbyists, corporations and the media
+ the importance of pressure groups as part of a pluralist society
+ arguments concerning the impact of pressure groups on democracy.

Exam practice

1 Explain and analyse three features of outsider groups. [9]
2 Explain and analyse three ways that pressure groups can influence government. [9]
3 'Pressure groups play a crucial role in the UK's democratic system.' Analyse and evaluate this statement. [25]

Answers available online

Check your understanding and progress at www.hoddereducation.co.uk/myrevisionnotesdownloads

10 The European Union

Key points

REVISED

+ The European Union (EU) consists of 27 member states.
+ Different EU institutions are responsible for executive (government), legislative (making laws) and judicial (interpreting and applying the law) actions.
+ The EU's aims include peace, removing internal borders, and achieving freedom and economic growth while promoting different cultures and languages.
+ Britain voted to leave the EU in June 2016, and left in 2020.
+ The EU has played a significant role in UK politics, both before and since the EU referendum.

Institutions

Key institutions

REVISED

Table 10.1 summarises the institutions that comprise the EU.

Table 10.1 EU institutions

Institution	Role	Significance
European Commission	Initiates EU legislation Drafts the EU budget and allocates funding Represents the EU in international negotiations	**Supranational body** 27 commissioners, one from each EU country Commissioners are not directly elected: national governments nominate commissioners and the European Council nominates the president of the Commission. Nominees are confirmed by the European Parliament
Council of the European Union	Main decision-making body of the EU (together with the European Parliament) Co-ordinates policies of EU nations Approves legislation from the Commission (as does the European Parliament) Approves the EU budget (as does the European Parliament)	**Intergovernmental body** Government ministers from each of the member nations attend and make decisions together Ten different types of meetings, attended by the appropriate ministers, e.g. finance ministers at the meeting on economic and financial affairs
European Council	Decides the direction of the EU and policy priorities	Intergovernmental body Heads of government (or state) for all EU nations meet four times a year
European Parliament	Approves legislation from the Commission (as does the Council of the European Union) Approves the EU budget (as does the Council of the European Union) Provides democratic supervision of EU institutions	The EU's only directly elected body 705 Members of the European Parliament (MEPs) Each EU nation is allocated a number of seats in the European Parliament that reflects its size, e.g. Germany has 96 and Cyprus has 6

Institution	Role	Significance
Court of Justice of the European Union (CJEU)	Judiciary of the EU Interprets the law and ensures it is applied in the same way across the EU Rules against EU nations that infringe the law Ensures that the EU acts appropriately and in accordance with its own laws	Judges appointed by national governments

The EU system of government (see Figure 10.1) features shared executive powers:
- the European Commission is the main executive branch
- the Council of the European Union also has some executive powers.

It also has shared legislative powers, exercised by:
- the European Parliament
- the Council of the European Union.

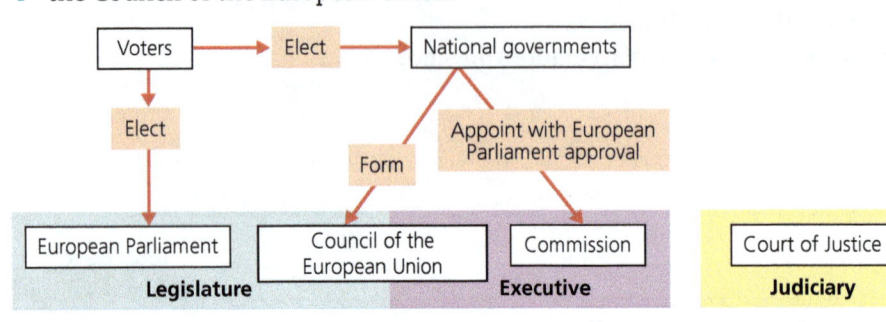

> **Supranational body** An organisation that exists separately from national governments. In the case of the EU, national governments agree to give power to its supranational bodies and to accept their decisions.
>
> **Intergovernmental body** An organisation made up of members of different national governments.

Figure 10.1 The EU system of government

The Court of Justice stands alone as the EU's independent judiciary.

Council of the European Union

- The Council of the European Union is made up of government ministers from member nations.
- It therefore effectively acts under the authority of the less-frequent formal meetings of the heads of government of the EU nations, which is known as the European Council.
- This means that both the democratically elected European Parliament and the democratically elected national governments have a direct role in the legislative process (see Figure 10.2).

> **Exam tip**
>
> Do not confuse the Court of Justice of the European Union with the European Court of Human Rights (ECtHR). The Court of Justice is an EU institution, whereas the ECtHR is not. The UK is no longer part of the EU but remains a signatory to the European Convention on Human Rights, so is still subject to rulings by the ECtHR.

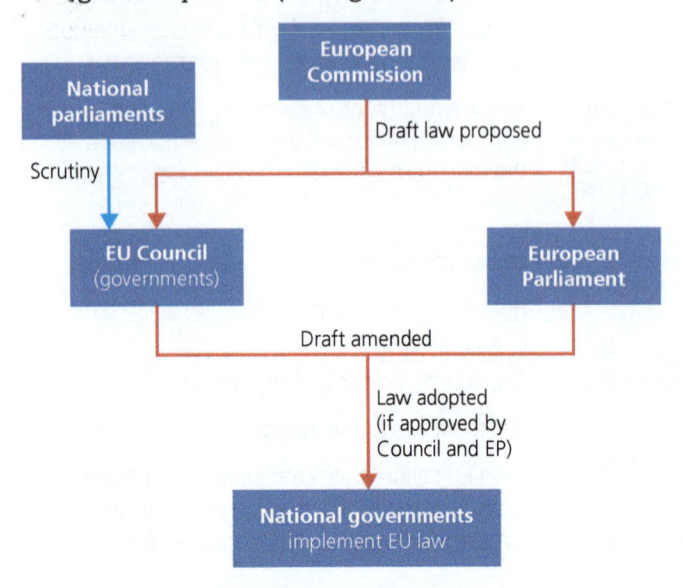

Figure 10.2 The EU legislative process

Check your understanding and progress at www.hoddereducation.co.uk/myrevisionnotesdownloads

The European Council

+ The European Council is responsible for making big strategic decisions (such as a change to a treaty or a major shift in policy direction), but it only meets a few times a year.
+ More routine decision making is carried out by the Commission and the Council of the European Union, along with the European Parliament when changes to legislation are required.

> **Exam tip**
>
> The Council of the European Union and the European Council are easily muddled up. The Council of the European Union is composed of government *ministers* and approves legislation and makes decisions on specific areas of policy. The European Council is composed of government *leaders* and is responsible for overall EU strategy, which is often determined by negotiations and bargaining between the most important EU members.

> **Revision activity**
>
> Make a set of EU institution flashcards. On each card, write a list of bullet points about one institution on one side and write the name of the institution on the other side. Test yourself by seeing if you can remember each institution from its bullet points.

> **Now test yourself** TESTED
>
> 1 Which EU institution has the power to initiate legislation?
> 2 Which is the only directly elected EU institution?
> 3 Which EU body is responsible for the overall strategic direction of the EU and is made up of the leaders of member states?
> 4 What is the name of the EU's judiciary?
>
> **Answers on p. 127**

Aims and achievements

What are the EU's main aims and achievements?

REVISED

The main aims and achievements of the EU are given in Table 10.2.

Table 10.2 Aims and achievements of the EU

Aims (taken and adapted from the EU's website)	Evidence that the aim has been achieved	Evidence that the aim has not been achieved
Promote peace, the values of the EU and the well-being of its citizens	+ The member nations of the EU have not fought each other since the end of the Second World War. + Rising living standards and economic growth have coincided with the EU's existence. + Democracy and the rule of law operate in EU countries.	+ The EU faces threats from an increasingly aggressive Russia, an unstable Middle East and home-grown terrorism. + The rise of populist anti-EU parties shows the frustration felt by citizens who feel the EU has not enriched their lives. The decision of UK citizens to leave the EU illustrated this. + The EU has been criticised for having a **democratic deficit**.
Freedom, security and justice without internal borders	+ All EU countries are part of the single market, in which the **four freedoms** apply. + 26 EU member states and European countries are members of the Schengen Area, in which there are no border controls between countries.	+ Not all EU countries are in the Schengen Area: the Republic of Ireland and Cyprus both chose to opt out. + Border checks can be reimposed by Schengen members in the event of a serious threat. Checks were temporarily reintroduced in 2020 and 2021 in order to protect public health during the coronavirus pandemic.

Aims (taken and adapted from the EU's website)	Evidence that the aim has been achieved	Evidence that the aim has not been achieved
	+ EU countries work together on policing and anti-terrorism, including using the European Arrest Warrant to arrest criminals across the EU.	+ Schengen states including Austria and Denmark have used border checks to stop migrants from the Middle East and Africa arriving via other countries in the Schengen Area.
Sustainable development based on balanced economic growth and price stability, and a competitive market economy with full employment and social progress	+ The EU has led the development of competitive economies, encouraging Eastern European countries to transition from communist states to flourishing capitalist economies. + The EU recovered from the 2008 crisis. Annual growth rates from 2014 to 2019 were around 2%. + EU environmental regulations are generally stricter than those of individual nations, resulting in higher standards of air quality, beach cleanliness and protection of species and habitats.	+ The 2008 economic crisis damaged the economies of EU nations, causing unemployment. Although they slowly recovered, unemployment remained high in some EU countries. + The coronavirus pandemic caused growth to shrink by 6% in 2020. However, the pandemic damaged the economies of all countries, not just those in the EU.
Combat social exclusion and discrimination	+ EU law protects individuals' human rights. + EU citizens have freedom of movement and cannot be discriminated against.	+ The 2015 migrant crisis exposed some of the prejudice within EU countries, demonstrated by attacks on refugee housing. + Various right-wing governments across the EU have restricted help for asylum seekers and migrants. + Far-right parties with anti-immigrant and anti-Islam policies have gained ground in many countries across the EU, e.g. Alternative for Germany (AFD).
Scientific and technological progress	+ The European Research Area encourages sharing of scientific knowledge, research and skills. + Billions of euros of EU funding are spent on science and technology. + The European Research Council's investments in scientific research have led to numerous breakthroughs.	+ EU countries invest less in research and development than their main competitors (e.g. China and the USA). + The USA is more effective at turning research and new technology into world-leading businesses, e.g. Facebook (now Meta) and Google.
Economic, social and territorial cohesion and solidarity among member countries	+ By **pooling sovereignty**, EU nations act as a united front. + The EU is the third-largest economy in the world. By working together, EU nations make better trade deals with non-EU countries than if they negotiated alone. + The single market is the largest in the world. It created more than 2.5 million jobs from 1992 to 2006 and has encouraged economic growth. + The EU protects workers' rights. + The EU provides hundreds of billions of euros of funding to less economically developed regions to try to reduce disparities across the EU.	+ Brexit was a huge blow to EU solidarity. + Strong anti-EU voices in other countries (e.g. Marine Le Pen in France) have called for their own referendum on EU membership. + The EU's goal of 'ever-closer union' has been enthusiastically promoted by France and Germany but criticised by leaders of some other EU countries, such as Italy and the Netherlands. + The single market has been criticised for over-regulating smaller businesses. + Socio-economic inequality is growing in the EU, as in many other capitalist economies.

Aims (taken and adapted from the EU's website)	Evidence that the aim has been achieved	Evidence that the aim has not been achieved
Respect its rich cultural and linguistic diversity	+ The EU has 24 official languages and provides funding for language learning. + Every year two EU cities are selected as European capitals of culture.	+ The EU has been criticised for its large expenditure on translation services. + The EU's goal that every citizen should speak two languages in addition to their mother tongue has only been achieved by about 20% of its citizens. + A number of EU countries have introduced a ban on face coverings worn by some Muslim women. In 2021, the European Court of Justice ruled that employers could ban employees from wearing the hijab (a headscarf worn by some Muslim women) in certain circumstances.
Establish an economic and monetary union whose currency is the euro	+ 19 member states (collectively known as the Eurozone) use the euro. + The euro is the world's second most-traded currency (after the dollar).	+ The 2008 economic crisis exposed the problems caused by a range of very different economies sharing the same currency. + This led to a long period of recession or near-recession for the Eurozone and forced austerity (cuts) in countries such as Greece, which fuelled the rise of populist anti-EU parties.

Democratic deficit The idea that the EU is not sufficiently democratic because most of its institutions are not directly elected.

Four freedoms The free movement of goods, services, people and capital within the EU single market.

Pooling sovereignty The idea of strengthening a country's resources by combining them with those of partner countries, giving the EU authority to make decisions on their behalf.

Making links

When the UK was an EU member, Wales was designated a less economically developed region of the EU, and therefore received hundreds of millions of pounds of EU funding each year. The rational choice model of voting behaviour might suggest that Welsh voters would have wanted to remain in the EU, but in fact 52% voted to leave in 2016. You can learn more about voting behaviour in Chapter 7.

Exam tips

The Schengen Area and the single market are not the same thing. All EU member states are part of the single market, in which the four freedoms operate. Most EU nations have also chosen to join the Schengen Area, a group of 26 European countries (22 of whom are EU members) between which there are no border controls.

Do not assume that the democratic deficit debate means that the EU is anti-democratic. The EU is based on democratic values: the European Parliament is elected and any country wishing to join the EU must be a democracy. The democratic deficit results from the way that many of the members of its institutions are selected by national governments. Institutions such as the European Commission and the Council of the European Union are not directly accountable to the electorate.

Although the EU has its own currency, the euro, EU member states do not have to use it if they prefer to retain their own currency.

Now test yourself

TESTED

5 Which of the four freedoms allowed high levels of immigration to the UK from EU countries prior to Brexit?
6 When was the last time that EU member states fought each other in a major war?
7 Which event caused unemployment to rise in many EU countries?
8 What are the economic advantages of EU membership?

Answers on p. 127

Revision activity

1 Give the EU a score out of ten for how effectively it has achieved each of the aims listed in Table 10.2.
2 Make a list of reasons to explain the EU's success or failure in achieving the aims given in Table 10.2.

The impact of the EU on UK politics

Cautious involvement: 1970s–90s

REVISED

- The UK joined the European Economic Community (EEC), the precursor to the EU, in 1973, some 15 years after it was formed.
- UK politicians remained divided over membership. The Labour government held a referendum in 1975, with the result that the UK stayed in.
- Labour later moved to the left and, in 1981, committed to leave the EEC if it won the general election (it did not). This prompted four high-profile members to leave Labour and form a new pro-EU party, the Social Democratic Party (SDP), which merged with the Liberal Party to become the Liberal Democrats in 1988.
- UK governments negotiated an EU budget rebate in 1981 and a selection of opt-outs from EU policies and treaties. These reduced the impact of EU membership on the UK compared to other EU countries.

Rising Euroscepticism: 1990s–2016

REVISED

- Conservative Prime Minister John Major (1990–97) found his government plagued by rebellions carried out by Eurosceptic Conservative MPs.
- The dominant political figure of this period, Prime Minister Tony Blair (1997–2007), was a Europhile, but the British political elite lacked the degree of consensus over membership found in most other EU countries. Eurosceptics existed in both the Labour and the Conservative parties.
- Tony Blair authorised the 2004 EU expansion, but the resulting high level of immigration from new Eastern and Central European member states was criticised by Eurosceptics and right-wing newspapers such as the *Daily Mail* and *The Sun*.
- The UK Independence Party (UKIP) was founded in the 1990s but grew significantly under the leadership of the populist Nigel Farage (2006–9, 2010–16), who criticised mass immigration, the democratic deficit and the bureaucracy of the EU.
- In 2014 UKIP won the UK elections to the European Parliament, pushing the Conservatives into third place.

Divided Britain: the 2016 EU referendum

REVISED

- In an attempt to prevent UKIP from taking votes from the Conservatives, Prime Minister David Cameron included an EU referendum in the Conservatives' 2015 general election manifesto. When the Conservatives won the general election, Cameron was committed to holding a referendum.
- The Tories were very divided over the EU: Cameron and many prominent Conservatives campaigned for Remain, whereas high-profile Conservatives such as Boris Johnson and Michael Gove played a leading role in the Leave campaign. There were divisions between Labour MPs, but most supported Remain. The Liberal Democrats and the Scottish National Party (SNP) both supported Remain.

+ Most 'expert' opinion (e.g. economists and business leaders) argued that leaving the EU would damage the UK. The Leave campaign was criticised for misleading claims about the impact of Brexit on the UK's finances. The Remain campaign focused on the economic risks of Brexit, rather than addressing voters' broader concerns by identifying the positive benefits of EU membership.
+ The final result—52% leave, 48% remain—was a terrible shock to many Remainers and highlighted divisions across the UK in terms of age, social class, education and geography (see Figures 10.3 and 10.4). Older, working-class, less-educated English and Welsh voters were each more likely to vote leave than those who were younger, middle class, university educated and living in London, Scotland or Northern Ireland.

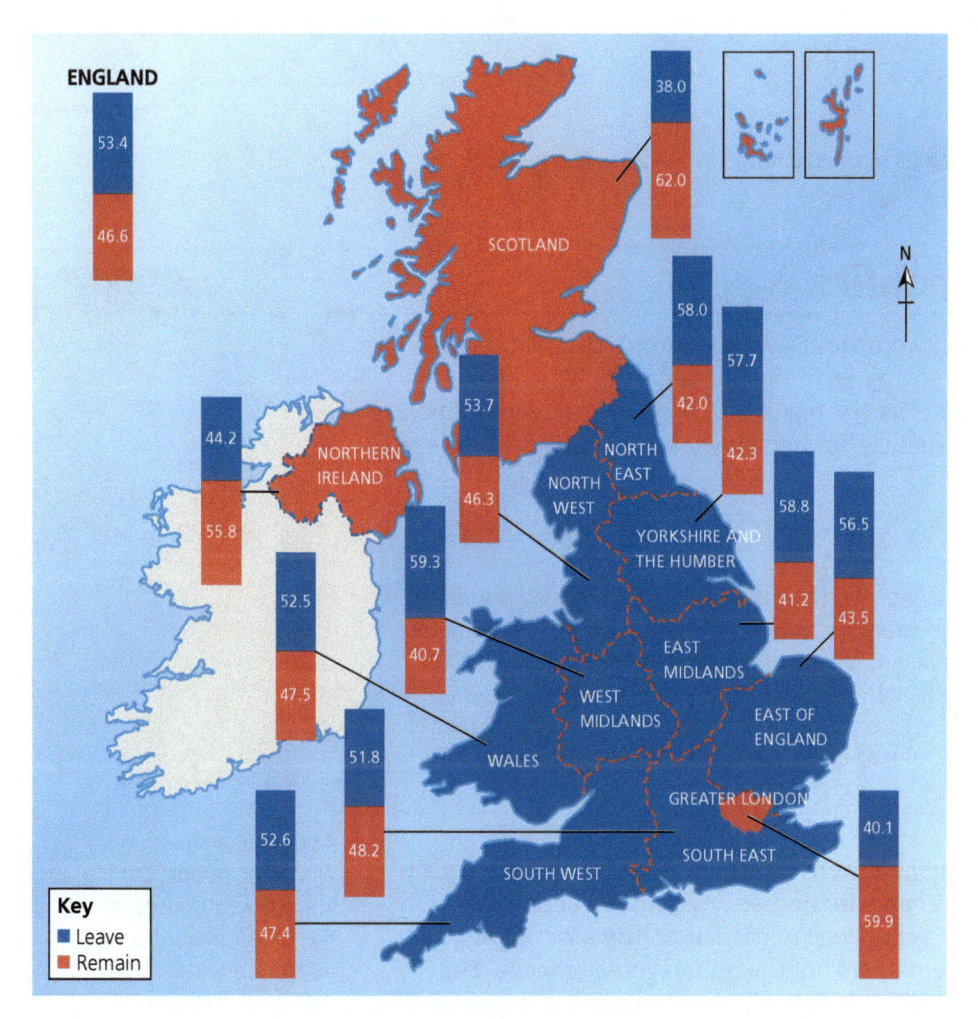

Figure 10.3 The 2016 EU referendum results
Source: Electoral Commission

> **Making links**
>
> One reason why the EU has had such an impact on UK politics is because it caused divisions within political parties and the creation of new parties. Internal division within Labour led to the 1975 referendum and the formation of the SDP, which became the Liberal Democrats. Internal division within the Conservatives resulted in Eurosceptic MPs causing problems for John Major and Theresa May. UKIP was set up to achieve UK independence and its successes drove David Cameron to commit to a referendum. You can learn more about the development of the parties in Chapter 8.

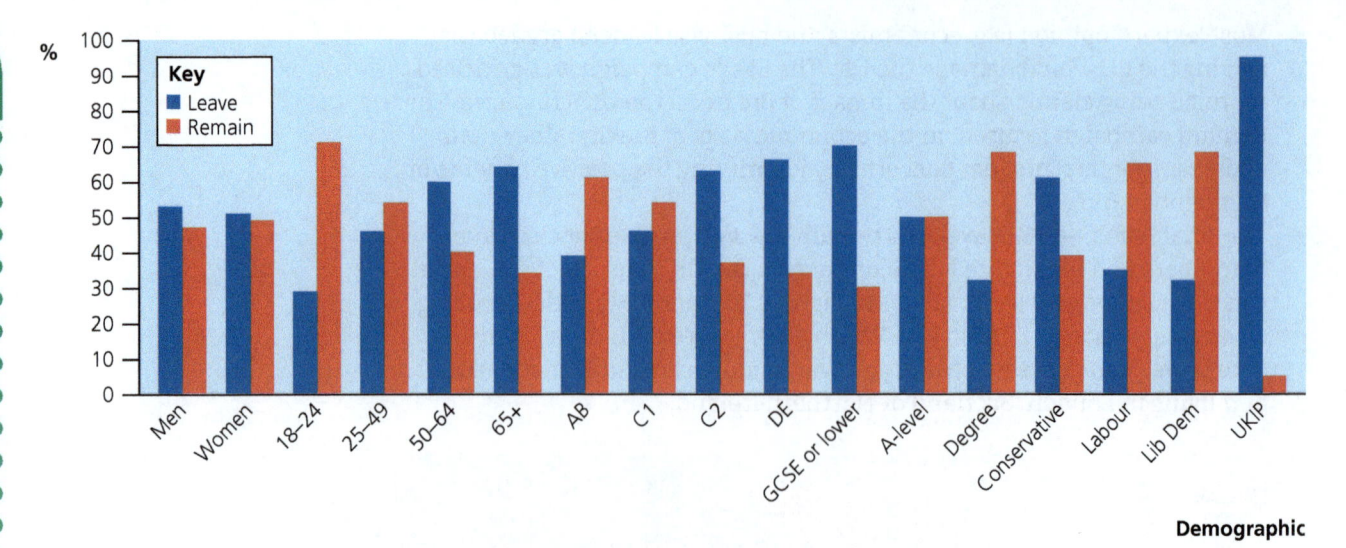

Figure 10.4 How different categories of people voted in the 2016 EU referendum
Source: YouGov

Post-referendum politics

REVISED

- The first impact of the Brexit vote was David Cameron's resignation as prime minister. After his leading role in the Remain campaign, he felt he could not carry on as leader after the result was declared. His replacement, Theresa May, was also a Remainer but had played a less-prominent role in the referendum campaign.

Making links

The Brexit debate had a significant impact on the UK cabinet. May included Brexiteers and Remainers in her cabinet in an attempt to maintain support from both sides of the party. Her reluctance to demote foreign secretary Boris Johnson after several high-profile gaffes demonstrated the extent to which her selection of cabinet ministers was constrained by Brexit. In July 2018, both Johnson and Brexit secretary David Davis resigned from the cabinet as they refused to accept collective responsibility for the government's proposed Brexit deal.

- The Brexit negotiations overshadowed all other political initiatives within parliament from 2017 to 2019 and dominated government activity.
- The referendum result was a challenge to parliamentary sovereignty, as the majority of MPs were Remainers but the nation voted to leave. The government had hoped to avoid asking parliament to vote on Article 50, but was frustrated by a January 2017 ruling by the Supreme Court (*Miller v Secretary of State for Exiting the European Union*). By requiring parliament to make the final decision, the Supreme Court made it clear that parliament is still sovereign, regardless of the referendum result.
- However, the majority of MPs ignored their own views and voted to trigger Article 50. This shows the importance of popular sovereignty in modern British politics.

Making links

Remainer MPs who voted for Article 50 because they believed the British public wanted them to were following the delegate model of representation. You can learn more about this in Chapter 2.

Popular sovereignty
Applies to a situation in which the people are the supreme authority and the government receives its authority from them. In theory, all representative democracies are based on popular sovereignty, as the people elect their representatives to act on their behalf. There is, therefore, only a tension between popular and parliamentary sovereignty when the people's wishes are different to those of their elected representatives, as in the case of Brexit.

- May lost her majority after calling a snap general election in 2017. Her minority government was dependent on support from the Democratic Unionist Party (DUP).
- Parliament was unable to agree on a Brexit deal, which eventually led to May's resignation in 2019. She was replaced by Brexiteer Boris Johnson, who also struggled to convince parliament to approve his deal. Johnson prorogued (suspended) parliament for five weeks in 2019, but the Supreme Court ruled this unlawful (in *Miller v The Prime Minister*).
- Johnson eventually called a snap election at the end of 2019. His campaign promise to 'Get Brexit Done' tapped into the Brexit-fatigue felt by many members of the electorate by this point. He won a large majority and passed his Brexit deal through parliament.
- The UK left the EU at the end of January 2020.

> **Exam tip**
>
> When revising, remember to reflect on the bigger issues at stake in the EU referendum. Parliamentary sovereignty was one of the main political areas of debate. Leaving the EU was said to restore parliament's sovereignty, as it removed the ability of the European Court of Justice to overturn UK laws if they conflicted with EU legislation.

> **Making links**
>
> The Supreme Court played an important role in protecting the rights of parliament during the Brexit process. The Court made it clear in the first Miller case that the government could not exclude parliament from the decision to leave the EU, and in the second Miller case that the prime minister's prorogation of parliament was unlawful because it prevented parliament from 'carrying out its constitutional functions'.
>
> You can learn more about the 2019 election in the case study in Chapter 7.

Brexit and devolution

REVISED

Brexit presents an ongoing threat to the future of devolution:
- Many political commentators and two former politicians, John Major and Tony Blair, warned that Boris Johnson's Brexit deal endangered the hard-won Northern Irish peace process.
- Within the deal, the Northern Ireland Protocol was designed to protect the Good Friday peace agreement by avoiding the need for border controls between Northern Ireland and the Republic of Ireland. The protocol allows Northern Ireland to remain within the EU customs union, provided it follows many of the same trade rules as EU countries. Some goods coming into Northern Ireland from the rest of the UK became subject to checks, however, to the deep disappointment of unionists. In 2021, the UK government threatened to suspend the protocol in response to the disruption caused by these checks and the Democratic Unionist Party threated to withdraw from government in Northern Ireland. The EU and UK negotiated to try to find a way of improving the protocol.
- The SNP have called for a second Scottish independence referendum as a majority of Scottish voters wished to remain in the EU in 2016.

> **Making links**
>
> You can learn more about the attitudes of Northern Ireland's unionists and nationalists to Brexit in Chapter 8.

The impact of the EU on UK policy making

Impacts on policy making

REVISED

Table 10.3 outlines some of the policy areas that have been affected by the EU.

Table 10.3 Impacts of the EU on UK policy making

Policy area	Impacts on UK policy making
Economy	+ The UK considered joining the euro currency under New Labour, but decided not to in 2003. This allowed the UK to retain its own economic policy, giving it some protection from the problems faced by the Eurozone after the 2008 economic crisis. + The UK was a net contributor to the EU budget, so UK governments had to pay more into the EU than they received back. + The EU negotiates trade policies on behalf of its members. Following Brexit, the UK has more freedom to make its own trade deals. However, it has less influence as it has a much smaller economy than the EU. + The economic disruption of Brexit unfortunately coincided with the economic damage caused by the coronavirus pandemic, requiring significant and widespread adjustments to UK economic policy.
Agriculture	+ The Common Agricultural Policy (CAP) provided EU subsidies (funding support) for all EU farmers. + The CAP prevented the UK from developing its own farming policies, which might have suited its needs better. Under the CAP, many wealthy UK landowners received funding and the system was criticised for promoting farming that damages the environment. + After leaving the EU, the government passed the 2020 Agriculture Act, which introduced a new system of public support for farming.
Fisheries	+ The Common Fisheries Policy (CFP) prevented the UK from protecting its fishing industry from competition. All EU commercial fishing boats had access to British waters, which damaged UK fishing. + Fishing was a thorny issue in the Brexit negotiations. The final deal was criticised by the UK fishing industry for not giving it full and unfettered rights to fish UK waters without competition from EU fleets. Since Brexit, there have been a series of arguments over fishing between the UK and other EU countries.
Environment	+ EU environmental laws forced UK governments to introduce more environmentally friendly policies, leading to lower levels of air and water pollution and the protection of species and habitats. + After Brexit the UK government introduced the Environment Act (2021) to replace the EU environment regulations that the UK had previously been subject to. It aimed to tackle air pollution and habit loss, and improve biodiversity.
Social policy	+ EU social policy led to increased rights for UK workers, e.g. paid holidays. + EU laws and initiatives to promote gender equality had a big impact on UK policy, leading to shared parental leave, the outlawing of gender pay discrimination and maternity discrimination, and funding for gender equality and anti-violence against women work. + Many commentators feared that leaving the EU would have a negative impact on future UK social policy. Brexiteers argued that there was no reason why Britain could not pursue similar policies alone.
Policing and security	+ EU membership allowed the UK to benefit from a co-ordinated policing and security strategy with other members, including a system of information sharing between national police forces and security services, and the European Arrest Warrant. + The UK lost access to these after Brexit, forcing the government to develop alternative arrangements.
Immigration	+ Freedom of movement prevented UK governments from restricting immigration from EU countries. In the year before the 2016 referendum, net migration to the UK from EU countries was around 190,000. + From 2010, the Conservative Party promised to cut net migration to 'the tens of thousands'. This was impossible to achieve as long as the UK remained in the EU. Johnson's 2019 manifesto promised an 'Australian-style points system' after Brexit to manage immigration. + Brexit gives UK governments more freedom to introduce immigration controls, but many experts argue that immigration is essential for the health of the economy. The combination of Brexit and the pandemic led to a serious labour shortage in 2021 in the catering and hospitality, agriculture, manufacturing, and transport, logistics and warehouse sectors.

Check your understanding and progress at www.hoddereducation.co.uk/myrevisionnotesdownloads

Post Brexit, the UK government is developing independent policies in each policy area. It has pledged to maintain many of the same funding commitments for the initial years after Brexit but, in the longer term, it will likely develop its own unique policies that may differ significantly from those of the EU.

Making links

All UK political parties have had to develop new policies in response to Brexit. The two parties most defined by the EU debate—the pro-leave Brexit Party and the pro-remain Liberal Democrats—face the challenge of creating a post-Brexit identity for themselves. The Brexit Party began this process by renaming itself Reform UK. You can learn more about both parties in Chapter 8.

Now test yourself

TESTED

9 Which UK political party has been most divided over Britain's EU membership?
10 What percentage of UK voters chose to leave the EU in the 2016 referendum?
11 How did the 2016 referendum result affect the leadership of the UK government?
12 Which high-profile Brexiteer was first given the job of foreign secretary in Theresa May's cabinet?

Answers on p. 127

Revision activity

1 Using Table 10.3, make a list of policies that were developed by political parties and governments as a result of the EU.
2 Make a note of the different ways in which the EU has affected:
   + political parties
   + government (including the role of the prime minister and cabinet)
   + the constitution (including the threat to devolution and the challenge to parliamentary sovereignty)
   + democracy (including the democratic deficit and popular sovereignty).

Exam skills

The EU topic requires you to understand two broad areas:
+ how the EU works—its institutions, aims and achievements
+ the EU's impact on the UK—both in terms of politics and policy making.

Make sure to cover both in your revision. When covering the impact of the EU on the UK, remember that this includes its impact while the UK was a member, and also since it left.

There are lots of opportunities to make synoptic links in an essay question about the impact of the EU. Brexit has affected every aspect of UK politics and government, so it links to every chapter in this book.

Summary

You should now have an understanding of:
- the executive power in the EU, which is shared between the European Commission and the Council of the European Union
- the legislative power in the EU, which is shared by the Council of the European Union and the European Parliament
- the European Council and its responsibility for major strategic decisions
- the European Court of Justice and its role as the EU's judiciary
- the EU's successes in achieving many of its aims, including peace, freedom, diversity and long-term economic growth
- events such as the 2008 economic crisis, the 2015 migration crisis and Brexit, which demonstrated some of the EU's limitations
- the EU as a divisive issue in UK politics, and the extent to which Brexit and its repercussions have dominated the political agenda since 2016.

Exam practice

1 Explain and analyse three ways that the EU has had an impact on UK politics. [9]

2 Read the following extract.

> 'The decision to withdraw from Europe after the 2016 referendum has the potential to be a major watershed moment [...] It might reshape British politics in many different areas—its political economy, its role in the world, its party system and its constitution. The most likely constitutional change might be the break-up of the UK. Brexit has further destabilised the union, increasing secessionist pressure in Scotland, raising the possibility of Irish reunification, enhancing support for Welsh independence, and accelerating the emergence of a new politicised Englishness. The new Disunited Kingdom has been on full display during the pandemic. A second possibility is that Brexit may mark a turning point in Britain's political economy [...] There is talk of a more active role for the state, in part spurred by the Conservative agenda of 'levelling up' to retain its new support in former Labour areas, in part by the demonstration of what an active state can achieve during the Covid-19 emergency. But to make these changes of direction, there would need to be political commitment to a fundamental broadening and deepening of the tax base, and some major institutional changes in the way policy is delivered; at present, there are few signs of either.
>
> A third possibility is that Brexit marks Britain's relaunch as 'Global Britain' [...] One scenario sees Britain inexorably edging back towards closer involvement with the EU and adopting the kind of associate status that Jacques Delors (former president of the European Commission) once urged the UK to consider. That is because the realistic possibilities for Global Britain outside the EU orbit altogether are not great. Britain will remain a strong supporter of the Western Alliance and the leadership role of the United States, but this was Britain's position before Brexit. Britain was always a reluctant and, at times, an awkward partner for Europe, but the relationship was an indispensable one for both sides. That has not changed. The British have won greater freedom of action in some areas by giving up the power to shape and influence the general direction of European policy, much of which Britain will still be obliged to comply with. Since Britain cannot just cut its links with Europe, the relationship threatens to be one dominated by friction and resentment.'
>
> Source: Andrew Gamble, Professor of Politics at the University of Sheffield and Emeritus Professor of Politics at the University of Cambridge, summarising aspects of his book *After Brexit and Other Essays* for the London School of Economics blog, 2021 (https://blogs.lse.ac.uk/politicsandpolicy/after-brexit)

Analyse, evaluate and compare the different arguments in the extract regarding the impact of the EU on UK politics and policy making. [25]

3 'Despite claims of a democratic deficit, the EU is a profoundly democratic organisation.' Analyse and evaluate this statement. [25]

Answers available online

Glossary

Term	Definition	Page
Access points	Points at which pressure groups can seek to influence decision makers. These include local government, devolved governments and legislatures, the UK government, parliament and the judiciary.	100
All-women shortlists	Lists of solely female candidates for a parliamentary constituency.	89
Article 50	The process by which a member state can leave the EU.	48
Asymmetrical	Uneven and not the same across the whole nation.	52
Backbencher	An 'ordinary' MP who is not a government minister or in the shadow cabinet.	21
Blairites	Labour MPs regarded as being loyal to Prime Minister Tony Blair during the Labour governments of 1997–2010. Peter Mandelson was a prominent member of this group.	35
Brexiteers	Those who supported the Leave campaign in the 2016 EU referendum.	35
Brownites	Labour MPs regarded as being loyal to Chancellor Gordon Brown during the Labour governments of 1997–2010. Ed Balls was a prominent member of this group.	35
Campaign	An attempt by a political party to persuade people to vote for its candidates or, in the case of a referendum, in accordance with its views.	73
Clause IV	Part of the 1918 Labour constitution, which committed Labour to the 'common ownership of the means of production, distribution and exchange', meaning widespread nationalisation. In 1995 Blair rewrote the clause, removing references to socialist economic policy.	74
Collective cabinet responsibility	The principle whereby all members of the cabinet support its decisions in public, even if they disagree with them in private and argued against them in cabinet discussion. It is seen as vital to the effective functioning of cabinet government.	33
Core executive	The collective term for the key players in government policy making. It comprises the prime minister, the cabinet and its various committees, the Cabinet Office and senior civil servants.	31
Crossbenchers	Non-party-political peers. In effect, they are independent members of the Lords; an example is the former top civil servant Lord Kerslake.	25
Democracy	A system of government in which the people have ultimate power. The term 'democracy' means 'rule by the people'.	56
Democratic deficit	The idea that the EU is not sufficiently democratic because most of its institutions are not directly elected.	111
Democratic legitimacy	The authority a body (here, the Commons) possesses if it is elected and accountable to the people via free and fair elections.	25
Direct democracy	A system of democracy in which the people make decisions, not the government. Votes take place on specific questions.	56
Disenfranchised	When someone's right to vote has been removed.	76
Entrenched or inalienable	Describes something that cannot be taken away, such as a US citizen's rights in their constitution to equal protection under the law.	17
Europhiles	Those who support the EU project and see the EU as a force for good.	82
Eurosceptics	Those who do not support the increasing powers of the EU and are suspicious and critical of it.	79
Executive	The government, comprising all ministers and led by the prime minister.	19
Four freedoms	The free movement of goods, services, people and capital within the EU single market.	111
Free vote	A vote when MPs are free to vote how they wish, rather than being instructed to vote a certain way by the party leadership.	28
Human rights	Those rights that apply to all people. They are absolute, universal and fundamental. They cannot be removed from anyone.	12
Ideology	Core political beliefs and ideas, e.g. liberalism, conservatism, socialism.	82

Glossary

Term	Definition	Page
Inner cabinet	A smaller, more informal group of senior ministers who meet outside of regular sessions of the full cabinet. It is often seen as the place where the real decisions are made.	33
Intergovernmental body	An organisation made up of members of different national governments.	108
Joined-up government	A policy to make different departments in the same government work together.	33
Legislation	The term for all bills that have successfully gone through parliament. A law or Act of Parliament starts off as a bill and only becomes legislation when it has received royal assent.	22
Liberal democracies	Types of representative democracy in which the rule of law is followed, the freedom of citizens is protected by the government and many different political parties compete freely to win power.	57
Lobbying	Attempting to influence the actions, policies or decisions of MPs.	25
Lord chancellor	The government's senior minister in charge of the law and justice, and a political appointment. Until 2005, lord chancellors also acted as the head of the judiciary and as the Speaker of the Lords. Today, those posts are held by others and the lord chancellor (Dominic Raab in 2022) is just a member of the cabinet and in charge of the Department of Justice.	45
Mandate	The authority, given by the electorate, to carry out a policy. A party that wins a large majority of seats in the general election can be said to have a strong mandate from the people.	25
Manifesto	A list of policy commitments released by a party before an election. Once elected, a government should deliver its manifesto.	12
Marginal seats	Those seats in which the MP's majority is small, meaning that it could easily be won by another party.	67
Monetarist economic policy	Economic policy that aims to keep inflation low by controlling the supply of money.	73
MPs	Members of Parliament, each representing a geographical area of the UK known as a constituency (650 total), who sit in the House of Commons. The average number of voters per MP is 68,000, although the largest constituency, the Isle of Wight, has over 100,000 voters.	13
National Audit Office (NAO)	An independent government body responsible for scrutinising the use of public money and ensuring it is spent efficiently and appropriately. It is essentially the government's spending watchdog.	41
Neo-liberal	A liberal ideology that promotes free-market capitalism.	82
New Labour	The policies and values introduced by Tony Blair after he became leader in 1994, which dominated until Ed Miliband became leader in 2010. New Labour accepted the capitalist economic system and focused on equality of opportunity rather than equality of outcome (giving people equal opportunities, but not an equal standard of living). New Labour was a 'catch-all' party with broad appeal to different social classes, including the middle class.	74
North Atlantic Treaty Organization (NATO)	An international organisation of 30 Western nations including the UK, the USA, Germany, France and Turkey. Members agree to collectively protect each other's security: an aggressive attack on one NATO member is considered an act upon all. All members are committed to spend 2% of their gross domestic product (GDP) on defence.	86
Off the record	When a minister or other politician speaks to a journalist on the condition of complete anonymity. Therefore, a story will refer vaguely to 'sources close to the prime minister' and not mention a name.	37
Old Labour	The traditional policies and values of the Labour Party. These include a commitment to socialism, nationalisation, the welfare state, high taxation and the redistribution of wealth.	84
OMOV	One member, one vote.	88

Check your understanding and progress at www.hoddereducation.co.uk/myrevisionnotesdownloads

Term	Definition	Page
One-nation conservatism	A version of conservatism that includes policies designed to benefit all sections of society.	82
Opposition	MPs and peers not from the governing party or parties. The term 'official opposition' applies specifically to the largest single opposition party. It has its own frontbench shadow cabinet who directly mirror and challenge government ministers, especially at PMQs. Since 1945 the official opposition has always been either the Labour or Conservative party.	21
Osmotherly Rules	Guidance given to civil servants and other government officials appearing before select committees. Various versions of the rules have been in operation since 1980, but they have never been formally accepted by parliament. The rules were most recently updated in October 2014.	29
Parliamentary democracy	A democracy in which the executive is not directly elected by the people. Instead, the executive is formed by whichever party has the greatest support in the legislature (parliament).	57
Parliamentary privilege	The right of MPs to free speech within the Palace of Westminster. They cannot be sued for slander or contempt of court. This is significant as it enables MPs to speak freely in parliament. One example was in July 2021 when SDLP MP Colum Eastwood used it to name 'Soldier F', a British soldier accused of involvement in the 1972 Bloody Sunday shootings in Northern Ireland.	13
Parliamentary sovereignty	The basis of the UK constitution. Parliament is the supreme authority in Britain. This means that parliament's laws cannot be struck down by a higher authority.	11
Participation	People's involvement in political activity. It includes voting, writing to an MP, joining a political party or pressure group, standing for office, protesting and signing a petition.	62
Partisan dealignment	The process by which the electorate has become less strongly affiliated to political parties. It is reflected by falling party membership numbers and an increase in the number of floating voters.	63
Party system	The number of significant political parties operating in a country. Party systems include one-party (e.g. China), dominant-party (e.g. South Africa), two-party (e.g. USA) and multi-party (e.g. many European countries using proportional representation).	95
Party whips	MPs in charge of persuading their party's MPs to remain loyal. They seek to do this by argument and sometimes by inducements, such as the prospect of promotion.	27
Peers	Members of the House of Lords, mostly life peers who have been nominated by political leaders over the years, along with 92 hereditary peers and 26 Church of England bishops.	14
Pluralism	Political philosophy that emphasises the benefits of many different groups influencing the decision-making process.	63
Political agenda	The political issues that are prioritised by political parties, the media or in general public debate.	87
Pooling sovereignty	The idea of strengthening a country's resources by combining them with those of partner countries, giving the EU authority to make decisions on their behalf.	111
Popular sovereignty	Applies to a situation in which the people are the supreme authority and the government receives its authority from them. In theory, all representative democracies are based on popular sovereignty, as the people elect their representatives to act on their behalf. There is, therefore, only a tension between popular and parliamentary sovereignty when the people's wishes are different to those of their elected representatives, as in the case of Brexit.	114
Populist	A politician who presents themselves as the true champion of ordinary people, defending their interests against the political elite.	82
Post-war consensus	The acceptance by both of the main political parties that Britain should retain the post-war settlement (the nationalised industries and generous welfare state first introduced by the 1945 Labour government).	82
Presidential democracy	A democracy in which the executive (government) is directly elected by the people.	57
Pressure groups	Organisations that campaign for a specific cause, such as a trade union or an environmental cause. Unlike a political party, pressure groups generally do not aim to win political power through elections.	15

My Revision Notes AQA A-level UK Politics Second Edition

Glossary

Term	Definition	Page
Primus inter pares	The traditional notion that the prime minister is merely the 'first among equals' among fellow members of the cabinet. In reality, modern prime ministers have far more power.	31
Redress of grievances	The right of citizens to get wrongs or injustices put right. For example, a constituent might try to get their MP to put pressure on a government department or local council to treat a complaint more fairly. An MP could also do this by asking a parliamentary question or possibly by attempting to bring in a private members' bill to address the issue.	25
Referendums	Direct votes in which the entire electorate is invited to vote on a single political proposal. This may result in the adoption of a new law. In the UK, they are normally used only for major constitutional issues such as EU membership (2016) or changing the electoral system to the Alternative Vote (2011).	19
Regional list	A proportional system in which seats are allocated from votes using the d'Hondt formula. A closed list system is used: parties rank their candidates in the order that they will be elected and voters simply choose a party. Regional lists were used in UK elections to the European Parliament before the UK left the EU in 2020.	68
Remainers	Those who supported the Remain campaign in the 2016 EU referendum.	35
Representative democracy	A system of democracy in which people vote for elected representatives. These elected representatives make decisions on the people's behalf.	56
Reshuffle	When ministers are moved around government departments; some will be promoted, some moved sideways and some sacked from government altogether. The most infamous reshuffle was carried out by Harold Macmillan in 1962 when he sacked seven cabinet colleagues, an event known as the 'Night of the Long Knives'.	33
Revolutionary socialism	An ideology that aims to create a socialist society through revolution.	84
Royal assent	The formal approval by the monarch of a bill that has successfully passed through parliament and that makes the bill into law. No monarch has refused royal assent since 1707.	22
Royal prerogative	The powers traditionally held by the monarch but now, in practice, the preserve of the prime minister. These include the power of patronage, being commander-in-chief and negotiating treaties with foreign powers.	12
Safe seats	Those seats in which one party has such a large majority that it is highly unlikely it could be won by another party.	67
Snap election	A general election that is held earlier than expected and typically occurs relatively quickly after being announced. A government may seek a snap election if it believes it can win a big majority. The Fixed-term Parliaments Act 2011 states that general elections should happen every five years, but a government can still trigger a snap election if at least two-thirds of MPs vote for it.	75
Social movements	Long-term campaigns for the improvement of an aspect of society. Examples include the labour, women's, environmental and LGBTQ+ rights movements, and more recent movements such as #FridaysForFuture and Black Lives Matter. Social movements are less structured and organised than pressure groups and may include pressure groups within them. For example, the environmental movement includes pressure groups such as Greenpeace and Friends of the Earth.	97
Spin doctors	Political operatives who shape a politician's message so that it attracts maximum positive publicity. Blair's New Labour was famous for its use of spin doctors: the best-known were Alastair Campbell and Peter Mandelson.	74
Stamp duty	A tax payable when buying property.	51
Supranational body	An organisation that exists separately from national governments. In the case of the EU, national governments agree to give power to its supranational bodies and to accept their decisions.	108
Tactical voting	When a voter does not vote for their preferred party because they do not believe that party can win. Instead, they vote for another party that has a better chance of winning. This may be to stop a party they dislike from winning.	67

Check your understanding and progress at www.hoddereducation.co.uk/myrevisionnotesdownloads

Term	Definition	Page
Thatcherism	Margaret Thatcher's distinctive brand of conservatism. It included a monetarist economic policy, deregulation of business and finance, privatisation of industry and restriction of trade union powers.	82
The Troubles	The period from the late 1960s when much of Northern Ireland was affected by terrorism including bombings and assassinations carried out by terrorists from both communities: Unionist/Protestant who wanted Ulster to remain part of the UK and Catholic/Nationalist who wanted a united Ireland. These terrorists belonged to groups such as the Provisional IRA or the Ulster Defence Association (UDA).	51
Third Way	An ideological compromise developed by Blair's New Labour. It was a balance between centre-right economic policy and centre-left social policy, which focused on social justice rather than a socialist restructuring of the economic system.	74
Three-line whips	Parliamentary votes when MPs must follow the voting orders of the whips. Failure to do so by a minister would lead to resignation or dismissal. Backbenchers who frequently rebel are unlikely to be offered posts in the government or on the opposition front bench.	28
Threshold	The minimum proportion of the electorate who need to vote 'yes' in a referendum in order for their decision to be implemented. The government decides whether to set a threshold. A threshold is not generally used in the UK, but the most notable exception was the 1979 Scottish devolution referendum.	79
Trade unions	Organisations made up of workers, which campaign for better working conditions.	63
Triangulation	Tony Blair's repositioning of Labour on the political spectrum, moving towards Thatcherism on economic policy but retaining traditional Labour social values.	84
Trident nuclear deterrent	Britain's continuous at-sea nuclear deterrent, which has been in operation since 1969. The UK has four nuclear submarines, one of which is always at sea. Even if all of Britain's land-based defences were destroyed, the Trident nuclear missiles could still be fired from sea.	86
UK Supreme Court (UKSC)	The highest court of appeal in the UK. It has the power to make judgments based on the European Convention on Human Rights (ECHR).	43
Unitary authorities	Where a single council carries out all the functions of local authorities, including major ones such as education and social care undertaken elsewhere by county councils.	52
Wasted votes	Votes that do not contribute to the election of a political candidate. This includes votes for losing candidates and those for a winning candidate that are in excess of the threshold required for them to win the seat.	67

Now test yourself answers

Chapter 1

1. Because parliament can leave the EU simply by repealing an earlier law and passing a new law, for example the European Union (Withdrawal) Act.
2. Parliamentary privilege.
3. One year (it was previously two years).
4. The Cabinet Manual.
5. No, but breaking one can often lead to a major crisis for parliament/government.
6. It is absolute, universal and fundamental.
7. It can be easily changed and reversed.
8. The Information Commissioner's Office (ICO).
9. Around 50%.
10. The European Convention on Human Rights (ECHR).
11. The House of Lords.
12. a Bill of Rights 1689
    b Parliament Act 1911
    c Act of Settlement 1701
    d Fixed-term Parliaments Act 2011
    e Magna Carta 1215
    f Freedom of Information Act 2000
13. a Individual, as this is about practising one's religious faith as many Christians disapprove of same-sex relationships.
    b Collective, as this is all about the rights of a group of workers as a whole.
    c Collective, as this is about the rights of a free press to publish stories they feel are in the national interest. Given its context, such a story would be very much in the public interest.
    d Individual, as this is about one person asserting their rights not to be discriminated against (although it could also be argued that it reflects the desire to enforce the collective rights of disabled people as a whole).
    e Collective, as it is about a group of parents demanding what they see as fair treatment for their children (although it also has aspects of the collective right not to discriminate on the grounds of gender).

Chapter 2

1. 650.
2. Church of England bishops.
3. Law-passing.
4. Select committees have general oversight of government departments whereas public bill committees oversee individual parliamentary bills.
5. Respond to it (within 60 days).
6. A leading MP from the opposition.
7. It is too adversarial and theatrical, with a rowdy and often boorish atmosphere.
8. It can lead to the downfall of the government.
9. Not that important; although it formally makes a bill into a law, it is purely ceremonial and a formality.
10. The second reading.
11. a Second reading.
    b Royal assent.
    c Committee stage.
    d Third reading.
    e Report stage.
12. An independent peer not belonging to a party group in the Lords.
13. No, but on average around 40% of recommendations are enacted by the government.
14. Commons Liaison Committee.
15. Parliamentary votes in which MPs must follow the voting orders of the whips.

Chapter 3

1. Weekly.
2. The prime minister.
3. Five.
4. 2010.
5. Harold Wilson.
6. Ken Clarke or Boris Johnson.
7. Priti Patel.
8. Brexiteers and Remainers.
9. Senior civil servants or heads of government agencies.
10. First among equals.
11. d, b, c, a
12. The poll tax.
13. Covid-19 pandemic—criticism from Dominic Cummings.
14. That they often failed to listen properly to advice/criticism, and acted too much on instinct.

Chapter 4

1. No, judicial independence refers to the absence of political interference and influence, whereas judicial neutrality is about judges' ability to handle all cases objectively and fairly.
2. Judges, especially those who sit in the UKSC, can be seen as unrepresentative primarily in the areas of gender, ethnicity and educational background.
3. *Ultra vires* is the term used to describe a government department or other public body exceeding its legal powers. It reinforces the notion that no one is above the law.

Check your understanding and progress at www.hoddereducation.co.uk/myrevisionnotesdownloads

4 2009.
5 No, judges for the UKSC are appointed by a special selection commission set up when a vacancy occurs. All judges though are appointed independently of political influence.
6 EU law deals with areas overseen by the EU, primarily trade and migration between EU member states. The ECHR deals more broadly with individual human rights and tends to attract more publicity and criticism as a result.
7 Strasbourg (France).
8 No, but it usually does. To defy the courts would be very controversial and, pre-Brexit, ignoring EU law could have led to heavy fines/questions over continued membership.
9 The UKSC must take into account ECHR rulings when hearing cases brought by British citizens.
10 There is no clear pattern. Some decisions have backed the government, others have gone against it. There is no strong bias either way.

Chapter 5

1 a False: those in Scotland and Wales have more powers than Northern Ireland.
   b True: Northern Ireland not only has a different electoral system (STV), but power needs to be shared between the two communities—unionist and nationalist.
   c True: there have been several acts that have transferred further powers to Cardiff and Edinburgh.
   d False: English councils lack real legislative or tax-raising powers.
   e True: Scotland and Wales both use the Additional Member System (AMS) whereas Northern Ireland uses Single Transferable Vote (STV).
2 Scottish, Welsh and Northern Irish MPs can vote on matters that affect only England, but English MPs cannot vote on the same issues that affect the devolved regions.
3 Large cities/urban areas.
4 English votes for English laws. It could be said not to have been successful as not only were early elections called in 2017 and 2019, but the Act itself was facing repeal in 2022.
5 One from: Greater Manchester, Liverpool City Region, West Midlands, West of England, Tees Valley, Cambridgeshire and Peterborough, Sheffield City Region, North of Tyne, or West Yorkshire.
6 Referendums.

Chapter 6

1 Rule by the people.
2 Representation, participation, accountability, legitimacy, rule of law, elections, smooth transition of power, civil rights, education and information.
3 Direct democracy allows people to vote on specific questions and therefore make decisions independently. In a representative democracy, people depend on their elected representatives to make decisions for them.
4 Two from: Switzerland (initiatives), USA (initiatives), the UK (referendums and petitions).
5 Advantages:
   + Elected representatives should be better informed on political issues than the majority of their constituents.
   + Elected representatives may be less emotional and less swayed by populist, short-term thinking.
   + It is faster and more efficient than direct democracy.
   + Representative democracy protects against the 'tyranny of the majority'—representatives should consider the rights of all their constituents, not just the majority.

   Disadvantages:
   + It is not a 'pure' form of democracy: the people's wishes may be ignored by their representatives.
   + People may participate less in politics if all the decisions are taken for them.
   + This can also lead to feelings of disillusionment with the political system and a lack of interest in political information and education.
   + Decisions taken without the direct approval of the people can be seen as less legitimate.
6 1928 was the first year that women and men both had the vote on equal terms. However, 18- to 20-year-olds could not vote until 1969, so you could argue that suffrage was not universal until then. If you are a supporter of Votes at 16, you might argue that Britain still does not have universal suffrage.
7 Votes for all men over 21, secret ballots, no property qualifications for MPs, pay for MPs, equal-size constituencies and yearly elections to parliament.
8 The Suffragists used conventional, law-abiding methods of campaigning, whereas the Suffragettes used militant action, including violence and arson. However, the Suffragettes were careful not to harm (or threaten to harm) people; they focused on damaging physical property.
9 Labour, the SNP, the Liberal Democrats, Plaid Cymru and the Green Party.
10 A move from traditional methods such as joining a political party, signing petitions and attending marches or demonstrations, to online methods such as e-petitions and social media campaigns. Membership of pressure groups has also increased significantly.
11 The process by which the electorate has become less strongly affiliated to political parties.
This is reflected by falling party membership numbers.

12 'Slacktivism' describes the tendency for people to participate in a superficial way by 'liking' or sharing political content online.
13 Labour, the SNP (2014–18), the Conservatives (2018–21), Liberal Democrats (2014–20), UKIP (until 2016), Brexit Party (2018–19).
14 85% for the 2014 Scottish independence referendum; 72% for the 2016 EU referendum.

Chapter 7

1 A plurality system. This means that whichever candidate wins the most votes, wins the seat: they do not need a majority.
2 Votes that are not used to win seats. They include all votes for losing candidates and votes for winning candidates in excess of the number that was required for them to win the seat.
3 The tendency of FPTP to exaggerate the mandate that governments actually have. For example, in 1997 Labour won 2.5 times as many seats as the Conservatives, but only 1.4 times as many votes.
4 A constituency in which one party has a majority so big that they are highly unlikely to lose the seat in an election.
5 One in which the winner needs to have a majority of the vote to win the seat.
6 A proportional system.
7 SV is used for elections for the mayor of London, directly elected metro mayors, and police and crime commissioners.
8 Proportional systems are likely to create a multi-party system as seats are allocated proportionally to votes, meaning that smaller parties will find it easier to build up a presence in the legislature. Coalition governments are likely.
9 Social class: working-class voters were more likely to vote Labour, middle-class voters Conservative.
10 Age: young voters were more likely to vote Labour, older voters Conservative.
11 Labour.
12 English rural areas and southern counties, 'red wall' seats since 2019.
13 Labour isn't working.
14 It was the biggest landslide by any party since the Second World War.
15 UKIP won 3.9 million votes but only one seat in the House of Commons. This shows that FPTP punishes parties that lack geographically concentrated support.
16 Brexit.
17 Three: 1975 EEC referendum, 2011 AV referendum, 2016 EU referendum.
18 When a government wishes to implement significant constitutional change.
19 The 2014 Scottish independence referendum: turnout was 85%.
20 The people had voted to leave but parliament is sovereign so had the final say, and most MPs were pro-remain. While many felt duty-bound to honour the wishes of the people, MPs could not agree on a Brexit deal until the 2019 election produced a parliament that better reflected the referendum result.

Chapter 8

1 Any three from: neo-liberalism, monetarism, deregulation of business and finance, privatisation of industry, restriction of trade union powers, assertive foreign policy.
2 Cameron led the party to become more socially liberal, and his government legalised same-sex marriage. However, many Conservative MPs voted against same-sex marriage, and still hold conservative social values. The Conservatives' so-called 'war on woke' highlights the reservations that many members of the party have about modern campaigns such as Black Lives Matter and the trans rights movement.
3 It forced them to abandon their policies of austerity and restrained government spending. Johnson's government dramatically expanded the role of the state. The furlough scheme and other economic support measures required the highest levels of government spending since the Second World War.
4 The Third Way.
5 Any three from: renationalisation of the railways and utilities, reversing austerity and increasing taxes on business to pay for the welfare state, removal of university tuition fees, a desire to avoid war or nuclear weapons.
6 Reversing Brexit.
7 Liberal Democrats.
8 Labour.
9 Conservatives.
10 Conservatives—wealthy individual donors, followed by companies. Labour—trade unions, followed by individual donors.
11 Short money.
12 Rupert Murdoch. He owns a wide range of media and both Labour and Conservative leaders have tried to win his support.
13 The Democratic Unionist Party (DUP).
14 UKIP: the UK left the EU in 2020.
15 Proportional systems.
16 2010–15.

Chapter 9

1 A political party contests elections with the aim of winning political power, whereas a pressure group seeks to influence those who hold power.
2 An outsider group.
3 A promotional group.
4 Two from: coronavirus PPE provision, coronavirus inquiry, scrutiny of government pandemic response (2020–21), sugar tax on fizzy drinks (2018), public consultation on opt-out organ donation (2017,

enacted in 2020), smoking ban in enclosed public places (2007), compulsory seatbelts (1991).
5. 2016 junior doctors' strike over their new contract.
6. Strength: direct action draws media attention to the climate emergency, and makes the urgency clear to the public.
   Weakness: headline-grabbing 'stunts' can alienate the public, especially if they are directly inconvenienced, e.g. by travel disruption.
7. Judicial review.
8. A background campaign.
9. Direct action.
10. Labour.
11. Activist lawyers used judicial review. The government's air pollution policy has been ruled in breach of the law on three occasions.
12. Marcus Rashford.
13. A think tank is a research organisation that exists to create ideas and policies. Unlike a political party, it does not seek to win elections or form a government to implement those policies. Instead, think tanks hope to influence political parties and the government.
14. Someone, usually a professional, who meets with influential politicians to try to convince them to support the aims of a corporation or pressure group.
15. Most big businesses and business groups in the UK campaigned for Remain.
16. Pressure groups allow many different voices from different sections of society to have influence in government, allowing power to be spread more widely.
17. The Conservatives.
18. Many pressure groups have far more members than the political parties do. They also allow people to participate in democracy at any time, rather than just during an election campaign every five years.

Chapter 10

1. The European Commission.
2. The European Parliament.
3. The European Council.
4. The Court of Justice of the European Union.
5. Free movement of people.
6. The Second World War (1939–45).
7. The 2008 global economic crisis.
8. Advantages include:
   - Single market: corporations have easy access to labour because of the free movement of people; the free movement of goods and services allows frictionless trade; free movement of capital allows investment in different countries by businesses and individuals.
   - EU investments support less economically developed regions.
   - The euro is a strong and popular currency.
   - Leverage in trade deals, as the EU is the third-biggest economy in the world.
9. The Conservatives.
10. 52%.
11. David Cameron resigned as prime minister and was replaced by Theresa May.
12. Boris Johnson.